How to be in

Life in the Political Shadows

How to be in Opposition

Life in the Political Shadows

Edited by Nigel Fletcher

First published in Great Britain in 2011 by
Biteback Publishing Ltd
Westminster Tower
3 Albert Embankment
London
SE1 7SP

Copyright © Nigel Fletcher and individual contributors 2011

Nigel Fletcher and the individual contributors have asserted their rights under the Copyright, Designs and Patents Act 1988 to be identified as the authors of this work.

All rights reserved. No part of this publication may be reproduced, stored in a retrieval system or transmitted, in any form or by any means, without the publisher's prior permission in writing.

This book is sold subject to the condition that it shall not, by way of trade or otherwise, be lent, resold, hired out or otherwise circulated without the publisher's prior consent in any form of binding or cover other than that in which it is published and without a similar condition, including this condition, being imposed on the subsequent purchaser.

ISBN 978-1-90727-808-2

10 9 8 7 6 5 4 3 2 1

A CIP catalogue record for this book is available from the British Library.

Set in Sabon
Printed and bound in Great Britain by
TJ International Ltd, Padstow, Cornwall

Contents

The Author
Acknowledgements

Foreword   xi
Dr Mohammed Abdel Haq

Introduction: Why Opposition Matters   1

1. Officially Powerless: 5
Being Her Majesty's Loyal Opposition
Nigel Fletcher

2. Into the Shadows   39
Gillian Shephard

3. The Corridors of (no) Power: 77
Office Politics in the Heart of Shadow Government
Nigel Fletcher

4. Leading the Opposition   113
Neil Kinnock

5. Painting Their Way Out of the Corner: 133
The Conservatives in Opposition
Tim Bale

6. Lessons for a Leader: Labour in Opposition   155
Greg Rosen

7. Ignored, Irresponsible and Irrelevant?:   173
Opposition MPs in the House of Commons
Philip Cowley and Mark Stuart

8. Voices in the Dark: The Opposition and the Media *Guy Black*	187
9. Revolutionary Foot Soldiers: A Researcher's Tale *Nigel Fletcher*	195
Endnote	213
Epilogue	219

For Morty

The Author

Nigel Fletcher is the founder and Executive Director of the Centre for Opposition Studies, and is currently researching a PhD thesis at King's College, London. Born in Portsmouth, he graduated from Queen Mary, University of London, and was awarded the Professor Lord Smith Prize for his dissertation on the role of the opposition. After a year as an elected students' union officer he worked as a researcher at the London Assembly, before joining the Conservative Research Department, where he was special adviser on education between 2004 and 2008. In this role he served four shadow Education Secretaries, including David Cameron. During this time he was also elected as a councillor in the London Borough of Greenwich, and is now deputy leader of the opposition there. He lives with his partner in Eltham, south-east London.

Acknowledgements

This book has been long in gestation. The seed of the idea was planted when, as an undergraduate, I worked part-time for David Willetts (then at the start of twelve continuous years in the shadow Cabinet). In 1999 his Centre for Policy Studies pamphlet *After the Landslide* provoked an interest in this neglected subject, and the daily experience in opposition made it all the more topical. I owe David a debt of gratitude not just for that, but for his help and encouragement to me since.

Gillian Shephard, with her book *Shephard's Watch* and her accompanying lectures at Queen Mary, University of London, bears some responsibility for turning my interest into active study, and I am delighted she has given permission for the relevant extract to appear here. Professor Ken Young at King's College London has been a patient supervisor of my ongoing PhD thesis, and a source of much sound advice over the years, as has Professor Nirmala Rao.

My friends and former colleagues in the Conservative Research Department deserve a special mention for having shared the highs and lows of life in opposition, providing me with support and much fun along the way. Of the shadow ministers I endeavoured to serve, David Cameron, Nick Gibb, Alan Duncan and Tim Collins were particularly kind to me, and it was an honour to work for them.

I am of course indebted most of all to the distinguished figures who have contributed chapters and lent their considerable weight of expertise to this book. They have done so generously and with an enthusiasm I had no right to expect. Neil Kinnock, in addition, remains a valued supporter as an

Honorary President of the Centre for Opposition Studies, alongside Michael Howard and Charles Kennedy.

For easing me gently through the publishing process I offer my thanks to Iain Dale and his team at Biteback, particularly Sam Carter, Hollie Teague and James Stephens. Many other people have provided help and encouragement for this project at various times, including Michael Cockerell, Emily Dover, Jane Enright, Nick Hillman, Lord Lexden, Lord Lingfield, Baroness Morris of Bolton, Professor Lord Norton, Ed Owen, Stephen Parkinson, Peter Riddell, Chris Skidmore MP, Peter Taylor, Annie Winsbury and Helga Wright.

My final thanks are to my partner Richard Tonge, my family and friends, for their tolerance during the whole process.

Nigel Fletcher

Eltham
January 2011

Foreword

Dr Mohammed Abdel Haq

Chairman, The Centre for Opposition Studies

The idea behind this book – a brief guide to different aspects of life in opposition in the UK – is simple enough. But the concept it seeks to explore is a more complex and much broader one. 'Loyal opposition' is a very British invention, and not just because the phrase was first uttered in the House of Commons. It stands at the very centre of the Westminster model of democracy, and without it the rest of the system simply cannot function.

If this sounds like an exaggerated claim, consider our recent experience of the 2010 general election. That event underlined to me the extraordinary strength of the UK's established democratic process and peaceful constitutional settlement. Although severely tested by an inconclusive result it was found to be more robust and secure than some had feared.

The election was full of elements which illustrate democratic freedom in action. The prime ministerial debates showed our political leaders not as our masters, but competing to be our servant, nervous and sometimes sweating as they sought our approval. And where else in the world would the chief executive of the country turn his motorcade around and spend forty-five minutes apologising to a pensioner for whom he had earlier shown contempt – a length of time some kings and presidents are not given?

When Parliament met for the first time after the election,

Labour's acting leader congratulated the new Prime Minister, but warned him that she and her party would be tough, would scrutinise the new government's actions, and be relentless in doing so. The political freedom which had allowed David Cameron and Nick Clegg to attack and finally displace the previous government was reaffirmed as the defeated party pledged itself to the task of opposition. The formal title which Ms Harman then held, 'Leader of Her Majesty's Loyal Opposition' encapsulates this idea: it legitimises dissent at the very heart of our democracy, but does so within a shared belief in loyalty to the Crown, and thus to the political system.

That fundamental loyalty is what ensured a peaceful transition of power. The acceptance by a government of its defeat is a blessing of the British system which we must not underestimate. As much as some people tried to portray Gordon Brown as clinging to office in the days following the election, the fact remains that as soon as a stable coalition agreement was within sight, he resigned. Not only was that a recognition of political reality, but it also chimed with an enduring British sense of fair play – that parties play by the rules and no one forgives a bad loser.

The speed of the transfer of power is brutal, but humbling. Throughout it, the wheels of the government machine carry on turning, with civil servants transferring their loyalty to the new administration with a degree of continuity and impartiality which amazes even those used to similar political systems. There is no more vivid demonstration of this than the way an incoming prime minister is traditionally applauded as he makes his way down the corridor from the front door of No. 10, by the very same Downing Street staff who an hour before have said farewell to his predecessor.

There is something hugely reassuring about that continuity. Throughout the drama of the election and the coalition negotiations, as the political fate of the nation was being decided and power hung in the balance, normal life continued.

In the cafes of Covent Garden people sipped their cappuccinos, around the country government agencies carried on issuing passports and paying pensions, and abroad the army carried on its brave mission. Crisis? What crisis?

In all too many countries, an uncertain election result could have been the cue for alarming and chaotic scenes. But there were no tanks on the streets during our transition, and the only people laying siege to government buildings were journalists. The ex-leader had not been accused of treason and his former advisers had not been rounded up by the new regime. The worst most of them will have suffered is the hangover after drowning their sorrows in the pub.

This peaceful settlement depends absolutely on the existence of a democratic parliamentary opposition. Without it, voters are denied a choice at elections, and a voice between them. A strong, viable alternative government prevents the untrammelled exercise of power, and even those who do not support all its policies benefit from its existence. Human rights abuses, corruption and intimidation all flourish in countries where dissent is suppressed. A system that not only tolerates but institutionalises dissent is a system that understands the true value of democracy.

In the pages that follow, we see evidence from leading academics and practitioners of the difficulties of opposition, its challenges and limitations. But underlying that is a positive message of the benefits this institution brings to our democratic way of life. For British immigrants like me, these traditions – of peaceful political change, continuity and constitutional stability – are amongst this country's most prized assets, and make me proud to be British. We should wholeheartedly embrace them, celebrate them, and do our best to promote them here and around the world.

'No government can be long secure without a formidable opposition'
Benjamin Disraeli

'Opposition is impotence and insignificance and people at parties asking you if you know Robin Day'
Sir Humphrey Appleby, *Yes Minister*

Introduction

Politics is about power: who has it, how they get it and what they do with it. All too often this means that academic study of the subject – and the attention of commentators and practitioners – is focused on government. Yet this is, quite literally, only half the story. Our parliamentary democracy is based on the principle of a House divided – between those in office and those who oppose them – but our eyes are understandably drawn towards those on the Speaker's right: to the Prime Minister, the Cabinet and the MPs behind them. When we do spare a thought for those poor souls opposite, it is usually only in the context of speculating about what they will do if and when they themselves move across the Chamber and take power.

Since my earliest days studying politics, this imbalance has struck me as odd. Opposition is not simply a state of limbo, a period of political impotence and irrelevance. It is an integral part of our constitutional system and the way it operates matters profoundly to our democracy. A government taking office is at its most potent in its early years, and the measures it enacts then have by definition been devised, planned and refined in opposition. Yet the study of policy-making often deals solely with what happens in office. Equally, the effectiveness of the opposition in Parliament and in the country has a significant influence on how the government of the day is scrutinised, but we rarely consider what makes for a good opposition. In both these senses good government – in the present and in the future – depends on how an opposition behaves.

This book is not intended as a definitive reference work on the subject. It cannot hope to match the breadth and depth of the thousands of books that have been written on every aspect of the conduct of government. What it seeks to do, however, is to consider some of the practical and political factors affecting the opposition in the UK, drawn from the experiences of the past. In doing so, it highlights most starkly the frustrations and limitations with which leaders of the opposition and their colleagues must contend. It is true that life in the shadows of politics can be miserable and depressing, and it is perhaps inevitable that those seeking office should be unhappy out of it. But like a prison sentence, separation from the levers of power should be punishment enough for politicians: the many further indignities and obstacles heaped upon them do little to aid their rehabilitation, and can actively inhibit them in holding the government to account. Does this serve our democracy well?

The chapters that follow present a range of different views of how opposition works. I outline how the role has become more formally recognised over the years, the limited support that is available, and consider how practical issues like lack of space and problems with office administration can have a real effect. Neil Kinnock and Gillian Shephard give compelling and fascinating accounts from the politician's perspective, whilst Guy Black adds his experience in dealing with the media and I give my own more humble thoughts on being a researcher in opposition. In their chapters, Tim Bale and Greg Rosen put many of these issues in their proper historical context, by examining the experience of the Conservative and Labour parties respectively, whilst Philip Cowley and Mark Stuart consider the behaviour of opposition MPs in Parliament.

Any one of these topics could fill a book in its own right, and I personally hope that in future they will. It cannot be right for opposition to remain a fringe topic, subsumed within the wider study of parliament and government, and our democracy (as well as the parties themselves) would benefit from further research in this area. Meanwhile, those who today find themselves grappling with the problems and limitations of opposition will find much in these pages to encourage them, if only by showing them that their experience is not unique.

1. Officially Powerless: Being Her Majesty's Loyal Opposition

Nigel Fletcher

'Being leader of the opposition is one of the most difficult jobs in government' David Cameron told the audience during his famous leadership speech to the Conservative Party Conference in October 2005. Although the line as delivered may have been a slip of the tongue (he apparently intended to say 'in politics'), it contained a basic truth. The leader of the official opposition now occupies a position outside the executive, but within the official British establishment.

We have now reached a situation where we don't think it the least bit odd that the leader of the opposition is paid an extra salary by the government he seeks to remove, and that his party is given public funds specifically to support them in the job of disrupting and obstructing the work of Her Majesty's government. It is as if they are, in the words of the film-maker Michael Cockerell, a sort of 'licensed court jester', not only tolerated but required to harass and poke fun at those in power.

This formalisation of the role has taken place gradually over many years, and to truly understand what it means to be the opposition today, we need to look back at how it came about.

Who pays the piper?

Whilst there has been a recognition of the role of leader of the opposition for at least as long as that of Prime Minister

(I would contend Henry, Viscount Bolingbroke, was perhaps the first), it was not until the twentieth century given explicit recognition by the state with the award of a salary. This was enacted by the Ministers of the Crown Act 1937, a piece of legislation aimed primarily at regulating the haphazard levels of ministers' salaries, including providing the Prime Minister with a higher salary (of £10,000) and a pension.

It states simply that 'there shall be paid to the leader of the opposition an annual salary of two thousand pounds', with the only condition being that such a person should not already be in receipt of a ministerial pension, in which case the salary would be reduced by the same amount.[1]

This was the first statutory recognition of the office, and so had to spell out exactly who that individual was. The Act states it 'means that member of the House of Commons who is for the time being the leader in that House of the party in opposition to His Majesty's government having the greatest numerical strength in that House.'[2] If any doubt were to arise as to which was the largest party in opposition, or who was its leader, the question would be decided by the Speaker of the House of Commons, whose decision would be final.[3]

The rationale for introducing the salary was set out by Prime Minister Stanley Baldwin during debate on the Bill's Second Reading, in which he claimed 'I regard it as my own child', having suggested it a decade earlier to his colleagues, after discussing it with friends in Canada:

> It seemed to me that the Labour Party in this country, playing the part it does, and being the alternative government, was very unlikely, from its constitution, to have many men in its ranks who could carry the responsibility of leader of the opposition and of the party in this House, without some kind of assistance

---

1. Ministers of the Crown Act 1937, clause 5 (The Parliamentary Archive)
2. Ibid. clause 10, section 1
3. Ibid. clause 10, section 3

or without undertaking some outside work, as I know has been done, to keep the home going while they devote themselves and their time to this task.[4]

Labour leader Clement Attlee himself was certainly grateful, recording in his memoirs that 'family expenses were increasing, and it was a relief' when the measure was introduced. He recognised its innovation, noting, 'this provision often causes surprise to foreigners, who think it strange that money should be paid to someone in order that he may effectively oppose the government of the day, but it is actually a recognition of the fact that parliamentary government depends on having an effective opposition and that the choice of a leader should not be restricted due to financial considerations.'[5]

Nevertheless it remained controversial, as demonstrated during subsequent parliamentary debates on the Bill. One Member stated he would oppose the clause on 'constitutional grounds', arguing that if the leader of the opposition was paid out of public funds 'he ought to be the servant, not of the opposition, but of the House of Commons' and that 'if he is leader of the Labour Party, and has services to render to it, he ought to be paid by the machinery of that party, and no one else.'[6]

Another opponent argued that it was 'clearly illogical' that the state should pay the opposition, and that whilst 'no doubt it is convenient for the government that the opposition should be organised in a particular way, and that it should have one individual at its head', it was not the government's business to decide such matters.[7]

The extent to which state resources shape and control the way the opposition goes about its work remains a valid issue even today, as we will see when we look at debates around

---
4. Hansard, 12 April 1937, col. 744
5. *As It Happened*, Attlee (1954), p. 81
6. Hansard, 29 April 1937, col. 615
7. Ibid. col. 620

'Short Money'. But the principle of paying the salary has never since been seriously challenged, and the leader is currently entitled to £73,617, which combined with his MP's salary brings the total to £139,355.

There were some reported murmurings of discontent by Cabinet ministers after 1997 when a pay freeze imposed on them by No. 10 meant that William Hague was paid more then them. But Ed Miliband avoided the same scenario by opting to match the 5 per cent pay cut which Cabinet members agreed for themselves in 2010. This means he now claims £132,387 – just below the Cabinet ministers' level of £134,565.[8]

Privy Council & royal recognition

Formal recognition of the leader of the opposition is not restricted to the award of a salary, however. As the leader of *Her Majesty's* Loyal Opposition, the post also enjoys favour from the Crown. A convention has now developed that the leader of the opposition should be a member of the Privy Council, mirroring the requirement for Cabinet ministers. This preferment has been somewhat disguised by the fact that many were already members, having served as senior ministers. In recent times, William Hague, Michael Howard and Ed Miliband had all previously been in the Cabinet. But for others, membership had yet to be conferred when they took up their new position.

David Cameron, elected leader on 6 December 2005, was made a Privy Councillor on 14 December, and was formally sworn in on 8 March 2006. Iain Duncan Smith – elected leader on 13 September 2001 – had his appointment announced on 18 September, following a Privy Council meeting held at Balmoral that day and took the oath on 31 October.

---

8. *Ministerial Salaries*, House of Commons Factsheet M6, September 2010; BBC News website 17 October 2010

In addition, both they and the leaders who were already Privy Councillors were summoned to see the Queen at Buckingham Palace some time after their appointment. David Cameron's audience occurred on 24 March 2006, and he made reference to the occasion whilst paying tribute to the Queen on her eightieth birthday:

> As one tries to explain what one is up to, one is acutely conscious that she has heard it all before and seen it all before. Her first Prime Minister was Winston Churchill. Her first leader of the opposition was Clement Attlee. I am the nineteenth leader of the opposition the Queen has had to meet; I am sure that, like others, Her Majesty has no doubt noticed that the number has increased all too frequently in recent years. However, she was, as ever, far too polite to point that out.[9]

Recent leaders have also been given the chance to say farewell to their monarch. Michael Howard was received by the Queen on 16 December 2005 'upon relinquishing his appointment as leader of the opposition'[10], and Iain Duncan Smith had been similarly received on 10 February 2004.[11] Interestingly, given the historical links between opposition leaders and royal heirs during the Hanoverian period, the Prince of Wales has also shown an interest in getting to know alternative prime ministers, and has granted several of them formal audiences over the years.

This recognition of the leader of the opposition as a senior Crown office is reflected in protocol arrangements at the Palace, with its holder invited to state banquets and formal events such as the annual Diplomatic Reception, and to 'call on' a visiting head of state during a state visit.

Other national occasions also show the leader of the

---
11. Hansard, 19 April 2006, col. 128
10. Court Circular, 16 December 2005
11. Court Circular, 10 February 2004

opposition receiving formal treatment. The annual Cenotaph service is perhaps the most familiar of these, providing the sombre sight of the main party leaders standing side by side. It is not without its controversies, though, as Michael Foot discovered in 1981 when his choice of attire was inaccurately dubbed a 'donkey jacket' by the press and widely mocked. Eyebrows were also raised in 2010 when Ed Miliband was relegated to third place in the line-up of those laying wreaths, whilst Nick Clegg took the position immediately after the Prime Minister. Although as deputy Prime Minister Clegg had seniority in the government, he was laying his wreath as a parliamentary leader, and should really have been out-ranked by the leader of the opposition.

Taking a back seat

One of the old jokes about loss of ministerial office is that its first symptom is getting into the back of a car and finding it doesn't move. Indeed, for most former ministers the jolt of losing power is accompanied by a renewed acquaintance with taxis and public transport as they lose their government cars and drivers. But this is one ordeal that a new leader of the opposition is nowadays spared.

When he lost office as Prime Minister in 1970, Harold Wilson announced he would resume driving his own car, a decision which reportedly filled his staff with unease, given that he had not driven himself in more than six years. But before he had the chance to get behind the wheel, a different solution was found. Labour's Chief Whip, Bob Mellish, had spotted Wilson standing in the taxi queue outside the Members' Entrance of the House of Commons, and was outraged that someone who had held the highest office in government only weeks before should have to endure such indignity. Mellish approached Conservative Chief Whip William Whitelaw to ask if the government might provide a car and driver for

Wilson. The suggestion was approved, and a car provided from the Government Car Service, with Wilson's previous driver, Bill Housden, again assigned to him.[12]

Since then, the provision of a car has remained the most obvious physical sign of the leader of the opposition's official status. Whilst financial assistance is paid directly to his party for them to administer, the car and driver are provided by the Government Car Service and administered by the Cabinet Office. This arrangement has not always been without problems, and in May 2003 it was reported that officials from the Cabinet Office had met with staff in Iain Duncan Smith's office to discuss his use of the car.[13] They apparently reminded the leader's office that the strict rules preventing ministers using their cars for party political or private purposes also applied to the leader of the opposition. A review by the Cabinet Office of drivers' logs is said to have shown Mr Duncan Smith used his car to travel to a Tottenham Hotspur football match, to the Conservative Spring Conference, and to take his children to school. Conservative and government spokesmen officially denied there had been a breach of the rules, but anonymous sources soon claimed there had been a 'ticking off' and a warning that further infringements would not be tolerated.[14]

A change to these arrangements occurred in 2006, when the Conservative Party opted out of using a government-provided car for David Cameron and chose instead to lease one at commercial rates. The reason was Cameron's desire for a more environmentally friendly vehicle, and the lack of agreement on a suitable option from the Government Car Service. It was reported that the opposition, along with other government car users, was offered a choice between a Jaguar and a Toyota Prius, the latter being the 'greenest' option. But

---
12. *Glimmers of Twilight*, Joe Haines (Politico's, 2003)
13. BBC Online, 21 October 2003
14. *The Times*, 22 October 2003

Cameron found it too small, complaining: 'My problem is that often when I go on tour, I have a lot of people in the car with me and I found on the tour when I used a Prius it meant we had to have two cars rather than one, so I don't think it would be very good for the environment.'[15] In the end he settled on a Lexus, which still had lower emissions than his existing government car, and seemingly provided him with enough room.

Despite the car being privately sourced, Cameron retained the services of a government driver. This became all too well known after the *Daily Mirror* published pictures of him driving the leader's briefcase, shoes and shirt to the Commons whilst Cameron cycled in.[16] In response to a parliamentary question in November 2007, a minister confirmed that the government 'provides a driver to the leader of the official opposition to support him in carrying out his official duties. The costs associated with use for non-official duties are met by the Conservative Party'. The same answer also revealed the government provided a contribution towards petrol costs, and that 'the hours worked by the driver are determined by the leader of the opposition's day-to-day requirements'. The monthly cost for the service was put at £4,027 (excl. VAT).[17]

Short of cash

A decent salary and a company car are all very well. But the most valuable part of the state's package of benefits for the opposition is the financial support provided to them (and other opposition parties) for their parliamentary duties, commonly known as 'Short Money' after Edward Short, leader of the House of Commons under Harold Wilson. The first announcement of the government's intention to introduce it

---

15. Sky News, quoted by Epolitix.com, 23 April 2006
16. *Daily Mirror*, 28 April 2006
17. Hansard, 26 November 2007, col. 16W

was the Queen's Speech of 12 March 1974, which stated: 'My ministers will consider the provision of financial assistance to enable opposition parties more effectively to fulfil their parliamentary functions.'[18]

Edward Short gave further details of the proposal in a statement in July 1974, telling the House that it was an 'immediate need' for the opposition to receive additional support 'if they are to play their full part' in Parliament. He referred to the fact that the previous (Labour) opposition had been supported by researchers paid for by the Joseph Rowntree Social Services Trust, but that more permanent arrangements were now required.[19]

Discussion with the opposition parties took place and progress was reported at a shadow Cabinet meeting on 26 February 1975, which noted some resistance from the parliamentary Conservative Party to the acceptance of such funds. This may have been linked to controversy at this time over suggestions by the government that parties could be given state assistance for their activities outside Parliament. That separate issue was considered in depth by the Houghton Committee, which did eventually recommend a system of funding to political parties, but with several members dissenting and amid press criticism, no action was taken.

The more limited 'Short Money' scheme proceeded nevertheless, and on Thursday 20 March 1975, the Commons debated a motion on 'Financial Assistance to Opposition Parties', on a free vote. In his speech proposing the motion, Edward Short set out the justification for the sums being allocated, with a formula including seats held by the party, as well as votes cast in the preceding election (on the basis this might indicate the level of correspondence they were likely to be facing). He explained the government were setting an upper limit of £150,000, arrived at by costing a 'modest

---
18. Hansard, 12 March 1974 vol. 870 c47
19. Hansard, 29 July 1974, col. 32

establishment' for the leader of the opposition's office and estimating the amount required for assistance in the whips' office, and for research assistance for frontbench spokesmen.[20]

How the funds were spent would be a matter for the parties themselves to decide, provided they were able to certify to the House of Commons' Accounting Officer that they were spent exclusively on parliamentary business. Short then reiterated the justification for the scheme in democratic terms:

> In these days it is becoming increasingly difficult for opposition parties to keep up with those who are backed by the vast resources of government, either in research or in administration. We believe that a healthy and lively opposition is an essential part of democracy, and we feel that our proposals will go a little way towards redressing the balance between government and opposition.[21]

In the debate that followed, many arguments were made against the proposal, some of which were very similar to the concerns raised in 1937 over paying the leader a salary – namely that the added cost associated with opposing the government should be borne by the opposition party, not the taxpayer. As Robin Maxwell-Hyslop put it: 'Political parties do not commend themselves to the electorate by failing to do their job of attracting financial support and asking that money should be taken compulsorily from the electorate at large.'[22] This was echoed by Labour MP Arthur Lewis, who observed that 'people who are poorly paid but perhaps paying tax and people who have spent their working lives in the trade union and Labour movement fighting and struggling against the Tory Party and fighting against the Liberal Party will now have to contribute through their taxes without having the

---

20. Hansard, 20 March 1975, col. 1871
24. Hansard, 20 March 1975, cols. 1871–2
22. Hansard, 20 March 1975, col. 1873

opportunity of passing an opinion on supporting the Tory and Liberal parties.'[23]

Supporters of the measure such as Liberal MP David Steel sought to defend it by drawing a distinction 'between the financing of political parties in the country and the financing of political parties in the House'.[24] But others took issue with this point, including Labour MP Arthur Lewis, who urged his colleagues: 'Do not let us kid ourselves: this is only the start.'[25] He went on to predict that the motion's statement that funds should be spent only in relation to 'the party's parliamentary business' would not prevent wider use, as 'a party's parliamentary business can be stretched to cover any sin one wishes it to cover'.[26]

Steel's case was also challenged by future Conservative Chancellor Nigel Lawson, who rubbished the distinction, arguing:

> It is nonsense for another reason. As the late Gertrude Stein would have said, a pound is a pound is a pound. If one gives a party a pound to help it with its parliamentary duties, it releases a pound that it has already to enable it to be spent on something else in the country at large. It is impossible to distinguish between funds for one purpose and funds for another. . . So we should not delude ourselves as to what we are asked to approve this afternoon. It is the whole principle of taxpayers' money, public money, for political parties in general as parties.[27]

There was some agreement, however, on the lack of resources the opposition parties had to conduct their duties. Douglas Henderson spoke of the 'problem of operating effectively in criticising the executive' and the 'vast bulk of detail which must

---
23. Ibid. col. 1879
24. Ibid. col. 1888
25. Hansard, 20 March 1975, col. 1879
26. Ibid. col. 1882
27. Ibid. col. 1902

be processed',[28] whilst shadow leader of the House John Peyton concluded that 'when dealing with matters inside the House of Commons, it is not an unreasonable requirement or hope that the opposition should have that modest equipment which will redeem them from being sentenced to total inefficiency'.[29]

In the vote that followed, opponents of Short Money included MPs from across the political spectrum, with some notable names amongst them – in addition to Nigel Lawson were Enoch Powell, Douglas Hurd, Norman Tebbit, Norman Lamont and Dennis Skinner. The motion was finally won by 142 votes to 47. Amongst those who turned out to support it were future Labour Party leaders James Callaghan and Michael Foot, future Speakers Betty Boothroyd and Bernard Weatherill, and future shadow Cabinet members including Tony Benn, Robin Cook and Michael Meacher.[30]

At the next meeting of the shadow Cabinet, it was agreed that a sub-committee chaired by Sir Keith Joseph, including Angus Maude and Sir Geoffrey Howe, should consider how the first batch of funds could most effectively be allocated.[31] The sub-committee reported back on 6 May 1975, having concluded that after the costs of the leader's and whips' offices had been met, only about half the money would be left for helping the shadow Cabinet. As they considered it difficult to give help to many frontbenchers individually out of this total, they decided that support should instead be provided through a strengthened Research Department. New members would be recruited and salaries increased, two measures which together were intended to raise the general quality of its staff.

The remainder of the funds were to be allocated to the establishment of a secretarial pool consisting of five secretaries, who would be allocated to work for specific shadow ministers 'on matters connected with the discharge of shadow Cabinet

---
28. Ibid.
29. Ibid. col. 1924
30. Ibid. col. 1931
31. Shadow Cabinet: Minutes of 55th Meeting, 26 March 1975 (Thatcher Archive)

responsibilities' – primarily routine correspondence[32] During the shadow Cabinet's discussion of this proposal, some members felt the secretarial pool would not meet their needs, and whilst the sums for the leader's office, whips' office and CRD salary increases were agreed, the issue of the secretarial pool and CRD recruitment were deferred for further consideration.[33] On 18 June, a modified allocation was approved, giving £50,000 to the leader's office, £17,500 for research and secretarial assistance to the shadow Cabinet, £13,000 for the whips' offices in both Houses, £30,000 for extra Research Department staff, and the remainder towards the existing Research Department costs.[34]

As this debate rumbled on, a politically awkward situation arose. Mrs Thatcher received a letter from Edward Short, expressing his concern at press reports that the money might be used to assist the Conservative Party outside the House. Mrs Thatcher had not seen the article, but felt Short 'might have been confused by the fact that the Research Department is physically located outside the Palace of Westminster'. She believed there would be no breach of the terms of the parliamentary resolution, as the cost of the Department's work on exclusively parliamentary business would still considerably exceed the amount of Short Money allocated to it.[35]

At the next shadow Cabinet meeting, the nature of the 'press reports' had become apparent, and Mrs Thatcher asked colleagues 'to take special care to ensure that classified papers were kept under lock and key, following the disclosure in *Private Eye* of the conclusions of the paper by Sir Keith Joseph and Mr Maude on the allocation of the Short Money'.[36] The coincidence of her colleagues' unhappiness

---

32. Shadow Cabinet: Circulated Paper (Joseph/Maude on Short Money), 6 May 1975
33. Ibid.
34. Shadow Cabinet: Minutes of 65th Meeting, 18 June 1975 (Thatcher Archive)
35. Steering Committee: Minutes of 26th Meeting, 12 May 1975 (Thatcher Archive)
36. Shadow Cabinet: Minutes of 62nd Meeting, 14 May 1975 (Thatcher Archive)

with the original memo and its subsequent leaking surely cannot have escaped her notice.

Short Money has remained the mainstay of official funding of opposition parties ever since, although the scheme has been modified several times. The amounts set in 1975 were uprated in 1978, 1980, 1983, 1985 and 1988 by amending the original resolution. From 1985, monthly claims were permitted, then in 1987 the maximum limit parties could receive was removed. In 1993 a new resolution was agreed, and periodic increases were replaced by an inflation-linked uprating system. At the same time, financial support for travel in relation to parliamentary business was introduced.[37]

Until 1999, the amounts received applied to all opposition parties, not just the largest one. But on 26 May 1999 a new resolution was agreed by the Commons, which introduced a specific allowance for the leadership of the official opposition. This was described as 'a separately identified sum specifically for the office of the leader of the opposition, in recognition of the constitutional role played by, and thus the specific demands on, the holder of that post'.[38] This was the first time since the introduction of the 1937 salary that specific additional financial support had been afforded to that office. In the same resolution, the value of the votes and seats elements of the formula was increased by a factor of 2.7. Both these changes were made in response to a report on party funding by the Committee on Standards in Public Life, and substantially increased the available resources to the opposition.

Today, the sums allocated to all opposition parties are paid automatically every month, as is the sum to the office of the leader of the opposition. Only the travel element has to be claimed directly by Members, usually monthly. The use to which the funds are put is not directly regulated, but

---

37. *Short Money*, House of Commons Library Note SN/PC/1663, 1 July 2010
38. HC Deb 26 May 1999 c428

parties must provide the Accounting Officer of the House of Commons (the Clerk of the House) with an auditor's certificate confirming that all expenses claimed were incurred exclusively in relation to the party's parliamentary business. This arrangement has been criticised over the years, with suggestions that it is not transparent enough.

In 2001, the Public Administration Select Committee (PASC) considered the Short Money model as part of its investigation into Special Advisers. The Committee reported that discussions had taken place over what constituted 'parliamentary business' but noted that a definition had been agreed between the House authorities, the official opposition, the Accounting Officer and the National Audit Office. The Committee noted that its witnesses 'thought there was room for more guidance' and that 'the official opposition and its auditors were unable to give a categorical assurance that its Short Money funding was used exclusively for parliamentary business'. It also expressed concern that a 'description of parliamentary business was arrived at, without consideration by the House'.[39] PASC concluded there was 'an urgent need for stricter regulation as to what Short Money may be spent on and more transparency as to how it has been spent'. In its response to this recommendation, the government acknowledged this point and made a commitment 'to work with the other political parties to achieve greater clarity and transparency' in the use of the funds.[40]

In 2006 the issue remained contentious, and a Labour MP sought information on various aspects of the scheme, including how many staff were paid under it. The then leader of the House Jack Straw's reply gave a useful current

---

39. Public Administration Select Committee, *Special Advisers: Boon or Bane*, 13 March 2001, HC 293 2000–01
40. Public Administration Select Committee, *Special Advisers: Boon or Bane: The Government's Response to the Committee's Fourth Report of Session 2000–01*, 18 December 2001, HC 463 2001–02

summary of the purposes for which Short Money could properly be used:

> Short Money is given to opposition parties to help them to carry out their parliamentary business. This can include research associated with frontbench duties, developing and communicating alternative policies to those of the government and shadowing the government's frontbench. There is specific provision for meeting costs necessarily incurred in running the office of the leader of the opposition. Each opposition party has to provide a certificate from an independent auditor each year to the effect that all the expenses claimed were in respect of the party's parliamentary business. No information is available to me about the number of staff employed by the leader of the opposition who are paid from Short Money.[41]

Whilst the coalition government has committed itself to reform the funding of political parties, the leader of the House, Sir George Young, has stated they have no plans to change the Short Money arrangements. In the current year 2010–11, the Labour Party is entitled to a total of just under £5.2 million of Short Money. This is comprised of £4.5 million of general funds under the seats and votes formula, £129,991 of travel expenses and £604,493 for the leader of the opposition's office. The next largest opposition party, the SNP, has a total entitlement of just £145,610.[42]

In a separate development, in 2000 a Policy Development Grant was introduced, payable to all parties with more than two MPs sitting in the Commons, to assist them in drawing up policies for their manifestos. This is worth just over £457,000 per year to the three main parties, and is administered by the Electoral Commission.[43]

---

41. HC Deb 19 July 2006 c428W
42. *Short Money*, House of Commons Library Note SN/PC/1663, 1 July 2010
43. *Party Funding, The Electoral Commission's submission to the committee on standards in Public Life*, October 2010

Parliamentary precedence

The source of all the opposition's claims to official recognition is, of course, its role in Parliament, so it is not surprising that there should be significant precedence given to them in the proceedings of the House of Commons (and the Lords, although I shall restrict myself to looking at the lower house).

The opposition's established role in proceedings is given physical form in the seating arrangements in the Chamber. By convention, the opposition parties occupy the benches to the Speaker's left, but it has become further accepted that the frontbench nearest the Speaker ('above the gangway') should be reserved for the official opposition, in the same way as the frontbench opposite is reserved for ministers. The parliamentary rulebook Erskine May states: 'The frontbench on the opposite side, though other Members occasionally sit there, is reserved by convention for the leading members of the opposition.'

This convention was tested in 1997, following the landslide Labour victory, and the election of an increased number of Liberal Democrat MPs. On the morning of 2 July, with debate on the Budget due to take place, several Liberal Democrats sought to occupy the opposition frontbench, and pressed their claim in Points of Order. Their behaviour brought this stinging rebuke from the Speaker, Betty Boothroyd:

> It is custom and practice that the opposition frontbench is reserved for the official opposition, and I shall see that that is maintained. It is also custom and practice that the area below the gangway is for the minority parties... I have never known grown-up people to behave in such a crass and childish manner. I think that it is time that Members of this House grew up. If they do not, I shall want to see the leaders of the Conservative and Liberal Democrat parties very soon. I hope that those Members

now on the opposition frontbench who are not members of the official opposition will do me the courtesy of removing themselves right now while I am on my feet.[44]

The Members concerned scuttled swiftly back below the gangway. But whilst this ruling set out the normal scenario for the opposition, as is so often the case it is the exception that proves the rule.

The Second World War was a unique period in the modern history of relations between the government and official opposition. With Labour ministers entering the coalition government in May 1940, the opposition ceased to exist in any way comparable to its peacetime equivalent.

Nevertheless, the parliamentary requirement for an opposition remained. With the Labour leader Clement Attlee taking a major role in the War Cabinet, it was thought necessary to appoint a nominal leader of the opposition from amongst those not holding ministerial office. Attlee describes how first Hastings Lees-Smith, then Frederick Pethick-Lawrence, despite being wholehearted supporters of the government, 'performed the duties of a leader of the opposition, asking questions as to the business of the House and so on'.[45] The conventional seating arrangements of the House of Commons also had to be adapted to accommodate the unusual situation. The Labour Party continued to occupy the opposition benches, but the opposition frontbench was filled by leading members of both parties.[46]

A contemporary account of this arrangement was provided in the diaries of Sir Cuthbert Headlam, an elderly Conservative MP returned to Parliament in a by-election at the start of the war, who noted on 12 June 1940:

---
44. HC Deb 2 July 1997 vol. 297 cc215–8
45. Attlee memoirs (1954)
46. Ibid.

The 'opposition' is lead by that poor, little creature Lees-Smith who takes himself very seriously. Apparently ex-ministers of all parties are permitted to sit on the front opposition bench and Eddie Winterton and Herbert Williams do so. I doubt whether I shall – at the same time it is silly not to maintain an active Conservative group...[47]

In the actual proceedings of the House, the official opposition is given precedence in debate, with the leader of the opposition given up to six questions at Prime Minister's Questions, and other shadow ministers by convention called for multiple questions at their departmental Question Time. They are also called upon to reply to ministerial statements, to speak before the 'winding up' speeches on Bills, and so on.

Government consultations

Opposition spokesmen also receive recognition in the form of consultation and briefings from the government on important matters of state. These usually take the form of discussions on 'Privy Council terms' whereby the oath the leader has taken binds him or her to maintain confidences imparted by ministers in this way. This happens on an ad hoc basis during normal periods of government, but becomes more frequent during times of national crisis and war.

With the collapse of the wartime coalition before the general election of 1945, the Labour Party once more became the official opposition, with Clement Attlee as leader. But despite the apparent normalisation of the adversarial party system, the continuation of the war against Japan and the possibility of a change of government before its conclusion meant that the opposition was afforded exceptional privileges by Churchill's government. The most obvious and

---

47. *Parliament and Politics in the Age of Churchill and Attlee: The Headlam Diaries 1935-51* (Cambridge University Press, 2000)

widely known of these was the invitation to Attlee to attend the Potsdam Conference alongside Churchill and his Foreign Secretary, Anthony Eden, in the interim between polling day and the counting of the votes in the general election.

In his memoirs, Attlee mused, 'I suppose that in most countries the idea that the two leaders in a hotly contested election should be able to meet again on easy terms and to co-operate, would seem strange, but we had so recently been colleagues that we experienced no difficulty.'[48]

There was, however, a degree of co-operation between the two leaders which went even further during this period, and which seems to have escaped public attention. Just a week after the Labour Party left the government, Winston Churchill wrote to Attlee to make a remarkable offer: 'Should you wish to share in our anxieties, though not in our responsibilities, in strict personal secrecy I should like to offer you facilities to see papers on the main developments in foreign affairs and strategy.'

The Prime Minster then offered to put a room in the Cabinet Office at his disposal, along with a member of Cabinet Office staff to act as a secretary.[49] He reinforced the generosity of his proposal with a surprisingly personal touch, adding: 'In addition I should be glad to offer you the freedom of my Map Room. This arrangement would carry with it the opportunity for conversations on these matters between you, the Foreign Secretary and myself whenever necessary.'[50]

Notwithstanding the ongoing war with Japan, offering a serving leader of the opposition this level of access to the heart of government was extraordinary. Perhaps sensing that acceptance might be seen as compromising the Labour Party as an opposition, Attlee replied on 1 June requesting permission to discuss the proposal with his colleagues. Churchill agreed

---

48. Attlee, 1954
49. Churchill to Attlee, May 1945 (PREM 8/309)
50. Ibid.

this, and at the same time issued the invitation for Attlee to attend the Three Power meeting at Potsdam to ensure 'the voice of Britain is united'.[51]

Having consulted with his colleagues, Attlee accepted both offers, agreeing that there was 'great public advantage to preserve and present to the world that unity on foreign policy which we maintained throughout the last five years'. He stressed his understanding that this would not allow him to quote publicly information he received, but suggested that the fact of the arrangement should be made public.[52]

Finally, Attlee volunteered a significant proviso not demanded by the Prime Minister, noting 'I appreciate that you have made this offer in view of the special conditions existing at the present time and that I should not base any claim to a precedent on the fact of its having been made.'[53] His inclusion in the delegation to Potsdam was of course publicised, but his suggestion that the same apply to the full extent of the arrangement was not, and the files do not seem to show how extensive his use of official briefings was during the relatively short period before he assumed office as Prime Minister following the election.

With Winston Churchill finding himself rather unexpectedly out of office, and with the war against Japan soon concluded, the boot was very much on the other foot, and the relationship between the two party leaders took a different turn. Just over a year later, in September 1946, Churchill asked to see the Cabinet Secretary, Edward Bridges. When they met, the ex-Prime Minister referred to the previous summer's exchange of letters, and indicated he intended writing to his successor about them.

He assured Bridges he had 'quite understood' that the Labour Party on assuming office had not wanted to offer

---
51. Churchill to Attlee, 2 June 1945 (PREM 8/309)
52. Attlee to Churchill, 8 June 1945 (PREM 8/309)
53. Ibid.

facilities to him and his colleagues. But in his view the position had 'since grown darker', and he felt the granting of such facilities should be again considered.[54] There was also an underlying threat in the approach, with Churchill hinting he 'may propose publication of his letter of 31 May 1945' if facilities were not extended.

Given the war leader's transatlantic links, it is perhaps not surprising that Bridges noted 'Mr. Churchill throughout spoke with a strong belief in the desirability of what I think the Americans call a "bi-partisan" attitude to foreign affairs in the present difficult times.' The leader of the opposition seemed slyly to suggest that being given access would lead him to moderate his previous criticism of the government, as 'if he had had fuller knowledge of the facts he might well have taken a different view'.[55]

This meeting was followed up by a fascinating exchange of letters between the former and sitting prime ministers. On 6 October Churchill wrote to his successor making explicit his threat to publish their correspondence of a year previously, in order that it 'be known how very different is the treatment we receive from that which was offered to you and your Party at a time when we had a large majority in the House of Commons and had expectations of securing a majority in the new Parliament'.[56]

In paragraphs of the letter marked 'secret' he then expressed concern that 'the European situation has deteriorated gravely' and referred to his belief that the UK was entitled to a share of the atomic bombs produced by the United States. On both issues he suggested he 'may' have to raise these points in open debate in the House before long. He concluded by claiming he was not making any formal request to be kept informed, or asking for 'any political or party favour'. But he felt the

---
54. Memo from EEB to Prime Minister, 24 September 1946 (PREM 8/309)
55. Ibid.
56. Churchill to Attlee, 6 October 1946 (PREM 8/309)

public should be fully aware of the fact that 'there is no kind of consultation or contact between His Majesty's government and the official opposition on foreign policy, peace negotiations or national defence'.[57]

The Prime Minister's reply was some days in preparation, and went through several drafts, with versions being sent to Herbert Morrison, Arthur Greenwood and Foreign Secretary Ernest Bevan (who was in Paris) for their comments. The final version sent on 9 October ran to six pages and was a fairly effective demolition of Churchill's case. First he dealt with the threat of publication of the 1945 letters, reminding Churchill that he had been quite willing for it to be published at the time, and didn't know why this was not done. He then highlighted his self-imposed condition that 'mindful of the constitutional position in this country' he had expressly stated he would 'not base any claim in the future on this exceptional concession having been made' and that he had expected Churchill 'would take the same line, if our positions were reversed'.[58]

He then dealt in depth with the general complaint that Churchill was being unfairly treated, by giving him a tutorial in the practice of opposition. In this, Attlee notes with some irony, 'I have had quite a considerable experience of the practice in these matters as from 1931 to 1935 I was deputy to Mr George Lansbury and from 1935 to 1940 I was leader of the opposition. I know therefore, what was the practice of your three immediate predecessors in office.'[59] The position he then recalls reads like a civil service precedent guide, and serves as a useful summary of the constitutional convention for government–opposition consultations as it had developed by the time war intervened. 'It was', in Attlee's words, 'as follows':

---

57. Ibid.
58. Attlee to Churchill, 9 October 1946 (PREM 8/309)
59. Ibid.

From time to time the Prime Minister of the day would ask the leader of the opposition to see him to explain some particular situation in order that he might come to an informed conclusion on his course of action in the House. On occasions the leader of the opposition would seek an interview with the Prime Minister or sometimes the Foreign Secretary for a similar purpose.[60]

There was never, he added, the kind of continuous consultation and access to papers which Churchill sought, and as such the Prime Minister concluded he had followed precedent.[61] He also suggested it would not be in Churchill's own interests for further contacts to be established, arguing that it 'would be inadvisable from the point of view of the opposition to go further than this, without placing on the opposition leader a responsibility that must remain with the government'. As an example he cited the fact that some foreign governments already believed speeches by 'eminent persons like yourself' had been made with the collaboration of government, and that greater consultation would make it almost impossible to convince them otherwise. Such an outcome, Attlee suggested, would 'cause you to impose upon yourself a most unwelcome restraint'.[62]

Attlee's riposte seems to have subdued Churchill, as in his reply the following day, he didn't re-engage in the argument about access, instead focusing his three-page letter on clarifying his stance on military matters.[63]

A few weeks later, Churchill made a more conventional attempt to test cross-party relations, writing from Chartwell that 'I wish to bring a delegation from the Conservative Party to meet you and any of your Ministers you care to have with you in the next week or ten days'.[64] In case Attlee should

---
60. Ibid.
61. Ibid.
62. Ibid.
63. Churchill to Attlee, 10 October 1946 (PREM 8/309)
64. Churchill to Attlee, 27 October 1946 (PREM 8/309)

be in any doubt about the importance of such a meeting, he added, solemnly: 'It is my duty to impart to you certain information which I have received which causes me deep concern, and involves the safety of the country.'[65] He still seemed to be trying to resurrect his own prime ministerial precedent, declaring that 'any information which you may think fit to give us would be treated on the principles set out in our correspondence of June 1945'.[66] Whilst he didn't elaborate on the subject matter, the record of their eventual meeting was filed under the heading 'Soviet Union (Strategic Interests and Spread of Communism)'.[67]

After the close co-operation of the parties during the Second World War, the government and opposition had now returned to more informal consultations, along the lines of what we might perhaps call (and Churchill would certainly hate us to call) the 'Attlee convention'. This has remained the basis of such contacts right up to the present day, but the way in which it has operated has varied with the personalities of the leaders involved. Certainly when Edward Heath was leading the opposition, the lack of personal chemistry meant he appears to have had little regular contact or private briefings with Harold Wilson. Douglas Hurd, who headed Heath's office, recalls 'Ted had no time for Harold Wilson – he thought he was a second-rate fellow, and he didn't trust him.' Harold Wilson reportedly felt the same about his opponent, and as a result there was 'pretty minimal contact'.[68] Nevertheless, Heath himself recalled meetings between him and Wilson did occur on some contentious issues:

> It's mostly behind the scenes ... you get a message from the PM saying 'we've got a problem here and I don't want to have to make a statement about it immediately but I'll let you know that

---
65. Ibid.
66. Ibid.
67. File note, 6 November 1946 (PREM 8/309)
68. Interview with Douglas Hurd, 28 March 2007

I can do it in two or three days' time, and if you want to have a chat now I'm happy', so I go along and say alright, if it ought to be held back, let's hold it back.[69]

In the 1980s, direct contacts between Margaret Thatcher and Neil Kinnock were infrequent, as he recalls later in this book. His meetings with John Major were more cordial, and during the Gulf War, frequent. On this issue the shadow Foreign Secretary, Gerald Kaufman, was also extended the courtesy of Privy Council briefings. He saw Foreign Secretary Douglas Hurd quite often during this period, although Hurd remembers that the pair of them kept the fact quiet. Their conversations included discussion of parliamentary tactics in order to maximise the chances of keeping the Labour Party in favour of the war, an outcome which the government considered very important.[70]

This easier relationship continued with Kinnock's successor John Smith. An insight into this relationship was provided during Major's tribute in the Commons following Smith's untimely death. The Prime Minister told the House:

> Inevitably, the Prime Minister and the leader of the opposition have to conduct business in private and on confidential matters. Whenever we did, I always found him courteous, fair minded and constructive, but also tough for what he was seeking and what he believed in. We would share a drink – sometimes tea, sometimes not tea – and our discussions on those occasions ranged far beyond the formal business that we were transacting. To the despair of my private office and, I suspect, sometimes of his, the meetings extended far beyond the time that was immediately scheduled for them.[71]

---

69. Interviewed by Michael Cockerell for *How to be Leader of the Opposition*, BBC (1999)
70. Interview with Douglas Hurd, 28 March 2007
71. Hansard, 12 May 1994, col. 430

Tony Blair and William Hague's discussions seemed to be slightly more remote, with Hague revealing at the time:

> He telephones me, sometimes I have to telephone him, about national security matters, about Northern Ireland matters – those areas where there is some common ground between the parties, there are of course conversations between the Prime Minister and the leader of the opposition.[72]

During the Iraq war, these usually private exchanges were brought rather more into the open, with Iain Duncan Smith going to see Tony Blair in Downing Street for a briefing and emerging to address the press outside afterwards. This didn't meet with universal approval, with some Conservatives concerned that it made their leader seem unduly subservient – 'like Blair's messenger-boy', as one put it.[73] Following this, consultations under Michael Howard and David Cameron returned to the more private nature of earlier times.

As well as briefings on security, terrorism and defence issues from the Prime Minister, there are other irregular contacts between opposition spokesmen and their ministerial counterparts. These can often be to secure agreement or concessions on legislation, but may be on other serious matters of public concern. One notable example within my own experience was on the issue of the government's child protection systems for banning individuals from working in schools. Following a high-profile scandal and urgent ministerial action to tighten the system in 2006, successive ministers gave confidential briefings to shadow spokesmen on the sensitive work to track down any individuals who may have fallen through the system.[74]

Whilst such briefings are essentially informal and ad hoc, the

---
72. Interviewed by Michael Cockerell for *How to be Leader of the Opposition*, BBC (1999)
73. Private source
74. Private source

run-up to a general election sees a recognised official process of government contacts with the opposition. It is widely accepted that the basis of this convention is the arrangements of 1964, when Prime Minister Sir Alec Douglas-Home authorised civil servants to hold discussions with Harold Wilson prior to the election of that year. Wilson disclosed the arrangement publicly in a statement to the House of Commons as Prime Minister in 1970, and confirmed he had instructed the head of the civil service 'that the practice of our predecessors in these matters should be followed'.

On that basis, academics know the convention as 'the Douglas-Home rules'. They have since become formalised and refined over many decades, notably when John Major agreed to extend the timeframe under which they can take place to eighteen months before the expiry of a parliament, to take account of elections frequently having taken place before a full term. The current convention is described in the draft Cabinet Manual thus:

> At an appropriate time towards the end of any parliament, as the next general election approaches, the Prime Minister writes to the leaders of the main opposition parties to authorise pre-election contacts with the Civil Service. For example, pre-election contacts were authorised from 1 January 2009 for the election held in May 2010... The meetings take place on a confidential basis, without ministers being present or receiving a report of discussions. The Cabinet Secretary, as Head of the Civil Service, has overall responsibility for co-ordinating this process once a request has been made and authorised by the Prime Minister. These discussions are designed to allow the Opposition's shadow ministers to ask questions about departmental organisation and to inform civil servants of any organisational changes likely to take place in the event of a change of government. Senior civil servants may ask

questions about the implications of opposition parties' policy statements, although they would not normally comment on or give advice about policies.[75]

The meetings are certainly useful for both sides, but the system is by no means perfect. When Michael Howard's shadow Cabinet began meeting civil servants it was three months after the Party had published its detailed 'Timetable for Action' at the Party Conference. At least one Permanent Secretary raised an eyebrow at the list of 'first month' commitments presented to him by shadow ministers, and expressed doubts about whether it would be possible to achieve them.

By the time of the 2010 election, the Conservatives had made much fuller use of the facility. David Cameron's establishment of an 'Implementation Unit' under Francis Maude meant there was a team tasked with drawing up detailed plans for enacting policy, and these were able to be discussed with civil servants. Much of this preparatory work was assisted by the new Institute for Government, an independent research foundation with close links to the civil service. Sessions were held with shadow ministers and current and former civil servants to enhance the formal 'Douglas-Home' meetings. The Institute also produced an excellent and detailed report by Peter Riddell and Catherine Haddon, which considered how the process had worked in the past and how it might be improved.[76]

Foreign recognition

One area in which the opposition's official status is more fully recognised is in the field of foreign relations. As noted before, the leader is invited to call on a visiting head of state

---
75. The Cabinet Manual Draft, Cabinet Office, December 2010, para. 60
76. *Transitions: Preparing for Changes of Government*, Peter Riddell and Catherine Haddon (Institute for Government, 2009)

at Buckingham Palace during a state visit, and to attend the banquet given by the sovereign in honour of the visiting leader. But there are further contacts which go beyond such courtesies.

Leaders of the opposition, as aspirant prime ministers, are understandably keen to prove their credentials as world statesmen. They will want to visit foreign countries where they hope to be received by heads of government and generally treated as though their opinions are of some present or imminent significance. The level to which this premise is accepted depends to a considerable extent on the host country's assessment of the likelihood of the leader gaining power. But when it does seem likely, foreign powers have their own interest in sizing up potential newcomers on the world stage.

Nowhere is this fluctuating process more fascinating than in the relationship between an incumbent British opposition leader and the president of the United States. The most powerful office on earth has an obvious fascination for the holder of one defined by its powerlessness, and successive leaders have sought to gain some reflected glory from the occupant of the White House.

Harold Wilson, in his first few months as leader of the opposition in 1963, lost no time in making the pilgrimage to Washington to see President Kennedy. His visit was not popular with the Prime Minister of the day, as archive papers now reveal. Harold Macmillan wrote a rather sniffy telegram to the British Ambassador in Washington, in which he remarked:

> No doubt Wilson will talk a good deal to everybody, including the President, about what he intends to do as Prime Minister. I will not comment on the propriety of this performance, but I think that you ought to warn the President that in my view Wilson has not found his feet yet. In any case I expect the Americans, or at least the minority who are politicians, will realise that they should not take Wilson's views too seriously.

The Ambassador duly reported back that he 'had a word with the President' and that Kennedy had told him he would assume anything said in their meeting would be used for political purposes by Wilson. The Ambassador then remarked on 'a marked lack of enthusiasm for the visit among the administration', before adding somewhat undiplomatically 'those who have already met him dislike him, and those that have not distrust him. I don't think we are in for a very happy four days'.

Later that year, Kennedy visited Prime Minister Macmillan at his country home, Birch Grove in Sussex, and stayed overnight. Wilson's staff contacted the American Embassy to try and arrange for him to see the President during his stay. The Embassy replied that it would be a matter for the British government, and the request was passed to No. 10. Macmillan must have enjoyed writing to Wilson to tell him that it would not be possible as 'the time for discussions will be very limited' and that 'President Kennedy's short stay is of course rather different from more formal visits of other heads of government'.

Wilson was not best pleased, and the snub was leaked to the *Sunday Times* where it appeared under the headline 'Mr Wilson will not meet the President'. The article reported that 'no request for a meeting with Mr Wilson has been made by President Kennedy, or by any of the senior officials travelling with him. They felt that this was a matter for the President's host'.

The next time Wilson met an American president was March 1964, when he visited Washington and called on President Johnson. According to the White House minutes of the meeting, 'the President told Mr Wilson he was glad to see him again and Mr Wilson recalled that he had last been in the White House in April 1963, though he had come to Washington since then at the time of the funeral ceremony for President Kennedy'. The two then had a wide-ranging discussion on issues from Cuba and Cyprus to nuclear weapons and British domestic politics. With an election not far off, and Wilson looking likely to win it, the 'lack of enthusiasm' of the Kennedy administration had to be overcome.

By contrast, Margaret Thatcher's accession to the Conservative leadership a decade later in 1975 left the United States distinctly underwhelmed. The US State Department had sent a memo to the White House reporting that Edward Heath had been 'unexpectedly defeated as opposition leader' but concluded 'It is doubtful that Mrs Thatcher will win on the second ballot. A more likely victor is popular Willie Whitelaw…'

The following week a contrite State Department reported that 'Margaret Thatcher soundly defeated four opponents to capture the leadership of the Conservative Party, replacing former Prime Minister Edward Heath'. The note then made the damning assessment that 'since no British general election is expected for the foreseeable future, US–UK relations are unaffected. To win a future election she will have to move an appreciable distance from her position on the right wing of her party'.

Nevertheless, when Mrs Thatcher announced she would be visiting the US that September and requested a meeting with President Ford, Secretary of State Henry Kissinger advised the White House that 'the Department endorses the request as being in keeping with our close relations with the British. I concur that an office call by Mrs Thatcher on the President would be appropriate and desirable'. The visit went ahead, and was judged a success by the British Ambassador to Washington.

Two years later, in May 1977, Thatcher met Ford's successor Jimmy Carter at Winfield House, the US Ambassador's residence in Regent's Park. White House records show President Carter was advised by his Embassy in London that:

> It is important for you to see Mrs Thatcher in London, perhaps for a 10-minute courtesy call. This will help to ensure that your

travel to the north of England is not read as unduly political in England, a country with a strong sense of 'fair play.' There is also a good chance that Mrs Thatcher will eventually become Prime Minister; this could even happen before her scheduled visit here this fall.

In the event, of course, Mrs Thatcher did not take office for another two years, during which she met Carter again in the White House, for a less successful meeting in September 1977. The records of this meeting are still closed, but historians at the Thatcher Archive conclude that Carter formed a poor impression of her, 'finding her outlook dogmatic and her manner hectoring'. Afterwards he reportedly instructed staff never again to schedule him to meet an opposition leader.

This clash could have seriously damaged US–UK relations, but by the time of Mrs Thatcher's election victory in 1979, a State Department memorandum advised the President that they believed 'the new PM to be a cooler, wiser, more pragmatic person now than the opposition leader you met in May 1977 or the dogmatic lady who visited you in Washington that fall'.

The battle for favour at the White House has been continued by every opposition since, with mixed results. Neil Kinnock was famously embarrassed by President Reagan, who turned an invitation to the White House into a poison chalice for the Labour leadership, ensuring that no TV cameras were admitted, and instructing his Press Secretary to brief that Kinnock had been berated by Reagan over his defence policy. A decade later, Tony Blair was given the red carpet treatment by President Clinton in 1996, but in 2004 Michael Howard's stance on the Iraq war resulted in him allegedly being told by President Bush's staff: 'You can forget about meeting the President full stop. Don't bother coming.'

That exchange may have marked a particular low point in relations between the shadow Cabinet room and the Oval Office, but by April 2009, with Howard and Bush replaced by Cameron and Obama, things were going much better. The President touched down in London for an international conference, but the leader's staff correctly pointed out that as an inter-governmental rather than a state visit, it would not be usual for opposition politicians to feature on the itinerary. That having been established, the invitation for Mr Cameron to meet the President achieved much greater significance. A quick handshake between the two would have been notable, but the White House went out of its way to boost the Conservative leader's status. Announcing the meeting to the Washington press corps before the visit, deputy National Security Adviser Denis McDonough put him in esteemed company:

> The President will have a series of bilaterals, including with Prime Minister Brown, with President Medvedev of the Russian Federation, and with President Hu of the People's Republic of China. He'll also, during that day, have important meetings with the Right Honorable David Cameron, the leader of the Conservative Party, and with Her Majesty Queen Elizabeth II.

The hard slog of opposition is fraught with indignities, and a constant struggle to maintain credibility as a serious challenger for power. Having the White House accord you the same level of importance as the Queen is, by any measure, a good day at the office. An opposition leader may not be completely without honour in his own country, but being honoured by those abroad is usually the best sign that you're close to power.

2. Into the Shadows
Gillian Shephard

The Rt Hon. Baroness Shephard served in John Major's Cabinet from 1992–97 and in the shadow Cabinet until 1999. This chapter is an extract from her book Shephard's Watch – Illusions of Power in British Politics, *which was published in 2000. Her unusually detailed consideration of the role of opposition helped spark my interest in the subject, and I am delighted that she has given permission for the relevant parts to be reproduced here. Whilst time has moved on, the lessons she draws from her experience remain very relevant today.*

For most politicians, the point of politics is the exercise of power, and some politicians see a period in opposition merely as a period of impotence to be endured until the next election victory.

Despite the importance of the opposition's role, it is an area 'relatively neglected by scholars', as Peter Hennessy observes in *Whitehall*. The reason for this is not hard to find: politicians want to govern. Few wish to dwell on the mixture of failure, humiliation and disappointment that is electoral defeat. Even fewer would admit to enjoying opposition. As Margaret Thatcher once put it, 'When you are in government, five years is a very short time. When you are in opposition, it is a hell of a long time.'

Yet there is a positive job to be done. Apart from playing its role in the democratic process, a political party can use a period in opposition to refresh its structures and policies, and to get back in tune with the electorate. It can introduce new people and thinking, and form new alliances. It is one of the disadvantages of the macho, confrontational nature of British politics that no one can say so, much less prepare for it while still in power.

Eighteen years is a long time in politics. The general election result in 1992, the problems of the Major government between 1992 and 1997 and, indeed, the consistent message of the opinion polls during that period, gave force to John Major's comment that to expect a fifth Conservative term in office was to 'stretch the elastic of democracy too far'. In political life, however, it is unthinkable for contingency plans to be made for what everyone strains to avoid, even when they can see that electoral defeat is on the cards. Operating at a high level in politics sometimes unavoidably militates against what would be common sense in any other situation. And the electorate has, on occasion, surprised the political establishment.

Tories out!

The mood in the country before the 1997 election was to get the Tories out as a first priority, notwithstanding party manifestos. The scale of the defeat in terms of parliamentary seats was enormous; in terms of actual votes cast, less shattering. Not surprisingly, the Conservative Party took some time to start functioning again as a political force.

In the days following the election, the media were triumphant. Had they not predicted this? Was it not time that the country rid itself of the wicked Tories? Was it not, yet again, '*The Sun* wot won it'? No less triumphalist were the opinion pollsters. Having been spectacularly wrong over the 1992 election, it would have been more than their business was worth to get it wrong again. The sun shone every day, the new Prime Minister and his untried ministers smiled untiringly.

More than one naive quality journalist opined that a new day had dawned for Britain.

Many who had not before been tried in opposition felt that to creep under an appropriately-sized stone might be the right response. It took a little time before we realised that losing an election is not only part of political life, it also presents challenges and even opportunities for renaissance. But in the early days, the overwhelming feeling was of powerlessness.

Adjusting to opposition

One of the first lessons we learnt in opposition was that all the support systems to which we had been accustomed vanished. I mused on this a few days after the election, as I waited in a queue behind some part-time catering staff for my new parliamentary pass. I had come back to the House of Commons after an audience with the Queen to hand in my seals of office. The Palace, of course, had met this particular situation before. Everything was handled with the perfect light touch. Back at Westminster, however, I had the strong feeling that we were in uncharted waters, which was strengthened by the number of new faces around the House, new Labour faces, mostly, clamped to mobile phones and pagers, and uniformly beaming. And they had reason to do so.

I crawled into the House. Everything looked the same, but somehow strangely unfamiliar. Our whips' office was now the opposition whips' office, located on the opposite side of the Members' Lobby. It was almost empty, with a few stray papers drifting about, and an almost palpable sense of Situation Vacant. I asked for a list of Conservative MPs who had been returned at the election, together with their phone numbers. 'Sorry, we don't seem to have one,' I was told.

I rang Central Office, to be told the same thing. 'Who did you say you were?' the voice enquired, not unkindly and rather accurately.

The mood was one of *nostra culpa*. It would have been hard for it to be otherwise, given the mood of the country, which was euphoric that we had gone at last, and the triumphalism of the new government at its victory after so long in the political wilderness. At first it was worse than that. It was as if, at a stroke, the Conservative Party had lost all the skills and experience that, collectively, we possessed, and in addition as if we had suddenly become invisible. Journalists who for years had besieged our offices to talk to us no longer quite recognised us in the street. Our views were not only not valued, they were not sought. For a short time, there was a collective crisis of confidence. Help and advice were available. Old hands at opposition, like Michael Heseltine, Norman Fowler and John MacGregor, had been there before. They told us that what we were experiencing was what we could expect. They gave good advice. The wisdom offered by Heseltine was that the only way to get attention in opposition was to issue a press statement every Saturday morning, and await press reaction on Monday. Fowler warned that we would find it hard work with little public reward. John MacGregor reminded us that the opposition during the previous Labour administration in the 1970s had kept the government up for night after night, with vote after vote, and that such persistence had worked in the end. While none of these scenarios was appealing, at least they reminded us that there is life, in government again, after opposition, and here were the living proofs. At the same time, we were learning at first hand why political parties strain every nerve to avoid losing elections.

A Major shock

The mood of Situation Vacant was heightened by the first shadow Cabinet meeting after the election, presided over by John Major. For many of us, it was the first time we had seen him, or each other, since the defeat. The mood, as can be imagined, was grim. For one thing, our numbers were sadly depleted by the colleagues who had lost their seats – Michael Portillo, Tony Newton, Roger Freeman, William Waldegrave, Malcolm Rifkind, Michael Forsyth, Ian Lang, James Mackay and Paddy Mayhew had all left. So many absences seemed more substantial than our presence.

Our collective mood was not enhanced by what we found on entering the shadow Cabinet premises. Almost none of us had known where they were or what they comprised. In fact, they occupy what was formerly the residence of the Serjeant at Arms, with an outside entrance into the Speaker's Courtyard. Inside the House, they are reached from the Official Corridor behind the Speaker's Chair, via a long corridor leading past the Table Office and the Foreign Secretary's suite. Upstairs there is a large conference room and a set of smaller ones, which had been used by John Prescott before the election and during the campaign. There were empty pizza boxes, drinks cans, overflowing ashtrays. It looked as if it had just been vacated by an occupying army, which in a way it had. None of us was in a mood to ask the House authorities why, during a six week election campaign, there had not been time at least to clean the rooms but it was a disgrace, nevertheless, and not boosting to our collective self-confidence. The insight it gave us into the eating and recreational habits of our predecessors was also deeply unpleasing.

On the day of the shadow Cabinet meeting we crammed into the shadow Cabinet room, with its broken lamps and spaces on the walls where pictures or charts had been hung. John Major was in a sombre mood and clearly did not want any kind of post-mortem discussion, although Virginia Bottomley, who had been consistently loyal throughout our period in government, delivered an impromptu lecture on the perils of disloyalty. She was heard out in a resigned silence. Then John Major said, as was evident to us all, that he would be standing down as leader, that he would be prepared to do Questions, and other parliamentary occasions until his successor was appointed, and that for the time being the rest of us should continue to hold our pre-election portfolios. With that he concluded the meeting, and we trailed out.

His reluctance to do anything other than the bare minimum was understandable. He would certainly have wished to avoid rows and accusations which, had he allowed the meeting to run, would undoubtedly have surfaced in the press the next day. He might have been unsure too of whether he could have avoided losing his temper in the presence of some colleagues whom he perhaps thought more responsible than others for our plight. He would have been conscious, as we all were, of the leadership ambitions around the table. Whatever the reason, the meeting was highly unsatisfactory, and gave no leadership for the period to come.

I consulted the Chief Whip, Alastair Goodlad. Always a man of few words, he pointed out that he was having to do double duty as shadow leader of the House, and the best thing all of us could do was to shut up, get on and leave him alone.

There were, of course, things to do. The new government, flushed with its triumph, announced even before the House had assembled that henceforth there would be only one Prime Minister's Questions per week, and that the Bank of England would become independent. Furious, we rang our usual journalists to make statements about abuse of Parliament. We could almost hear their '*so what?*' shrugs over the phone. Hey, we were in new territory, man. All that stuff about Parliament had no place in the exciting world of New Labour. There had been a press conference, had there not?

There was a Queen's Speech. No one wanted to hear what we thought about it. John Major did a manful job in his response. We sat behind, the new invisible army as far as the media and public were concerned.

As was their right, the new government was determined to make an impact. They planned to make an announcement a day for months, not often including the House of Commons in their list of announcement venues. There was early education legislation. I was not helped by the fact that exhaustion and the election campaign had left me with a raging ear infection, which not only made me ill but also picturesquely deaf. Former education colleagues, notably Cheryl Gillan and James Paice, with our adviser, Elizabeth Cottrell, now unemployed, met in Cheryl's Millbank office to draft amendments and plan tactics for the forthcoming debates on the Bill in the House. It was a revelation of the resilience of these colleagues, and the newly elected Members of Parliament we drew in, to see how they tackled the work with no help, no resources, and no Party back-up. In some ways it was refreshing to work on our own, with no lines to take, no question and answer briefing, just our own views and convictions. We spent a little time laughing about how new ministers were currently being overbriefed and overcircumscribed, just as we had been, by the same officials who had worked with us.

Given the small size of the new Parliamentary Party, I felt we must draw in new MPs to help. We needed them, and they needed to get stuck in early. We got them over to Millbank, and trained them in how to intervene, ask questions, and translate such briefings as we had into parliamentary-style speeches. These new Members were wonderful – fresh, inventive and courageous. They were also constructive about the task in hand. After all, opposition was all they had known. I began to see positive possibilities about our changed role. Among the most outstanding in those early days were Theresa May, MP for Maidenhead, who had come into the House with a strong background as an effective councillor, Nick St Aubyn and Graham Brady. Keith Simpson also made a strong impact. We made sure that they would not be cowed by the inevitably hostile parliamentary atmosphere. They were not, and under Cheryl Gillan's leadership, actually kept the House up until the small hours, with relentless questioning on the Bill. They did rather better than I, as I succumbed to my deafness before the parliamentary process was completed.

There were all the usual irritations to be experienced at the start of a new parliament. This time, we were not in charge. Thus every change, every development seemed to be one designed to put us in our new-found place, the No Lobby.

One of the sillier nuisances that attends new sessions of parliament is the battle for the allocation of rooms. It is well known that new MPs have to wait up to a month before they are allocated a room. Until that happy moment, you trail around carrying mountains of mail, leaving it in unsuitable places and grabbing the chance to use a telephone when one becomes free. What is less publicised is the reason for this delay, which is that senior MPs are negotiating with the whips for their own rooms, changing their minds, throwing tantrums, and generally being grand, so that those lower in the pecking order have no choice but to wait their turn.

Each generation of new Members is routinely outraged by this treatment, especially those who have come from exalted positions in the private sector or local government – academics, of course, are used to scrabbling for space. 'Don't you know who I am?' or 'I haven't been treated like this since I was at university', are the repeated cries one hears at these times. The more people complain, the more grimly determined are the whips to exercise their power as parliamentary disciplinarians – in other words they start as they mean to go on. I remember being ridiculously pleased when I was finally allocated a coat peg in the Members' Cloakroom, and even more delighted when, in advance of actually having a chair and a desk, I was given a locker and key in the Library Corridor. Ken Livingstone, who entered the House in 1987 when I did, famously was not given a room, desk or phone for at least a year after his election. The whips, who decided to treat him in that way no doubt to teach him some humility, as they thought, must since have wondered if their tactics were a success.

The situation, of course, is much worse when a party goes into opposition. In our case, in 1997, the whip who had done our room negotiations before the election, the genial Derek Conway, had lost his seat and with him had gone the folk memory and bargaining positions. I was given a tiny room in which no more than six people could stand at once. I knew better than to complain: instead I fixed a meeting for fifteen people, among them the new (and until then stupidly intransigent) accommodation whip. He and ten or so others had to stand in the corridor, unable to hear what was going on. Curiously, and with no more being said, I was given a larger room. Others had a similar experience. The feeling of rootlessness it engendered permeated the Parliamentary Party through to secretaries and helpers. While these kinds of matters are trivial, and soon forgotten once a parliament gets under way, they are undoubtedly worse when a Party is newly in opposition. Everything seems designed to underline one's powerlessness.

Renewing the Party

An analysis of the 1997 defeat indicated that we needed to modernise the Party, to get back in touch with the electorate, and to renew our policy base. We were powerless as politicians for the moment, but we could at least achieve change in those areas we controlled.

After his election as leader, William Hague addressed a large meeting of the Conservative Party at Central Office early in July 1997. He said, 'Political parties do not succeed through good organisation alone. But they certainly do not succeed without one.' He went on to describe how the Party had declined throughout his lifetime, and pointed out that the average age of members was sixty-four. He said that the local government base had thinned, and the number of professional Party agents who organised the Party associations in the constituencies had halved since 1970. In launching a programme for renewal and reform of the Conservative Party, he said, 'Our current organisation is not up to the job. No change is not an option. We need to renew our organisation, rebuild our membership and rejuvenate our Party if we are once again to become the dominant political force in the land.'

For the past eighteen years, we had been busy governing and it would be no exaggeration to say that we had lost touch with many of the changes affecting the lives of the electorate, some of which were the result of our own policy successes. The Labour Party in opposition had had the time to take account of these changes, and used them to their advantage. Their vocabulary, of 'new' and 'modern', chimed with the voters of 1997.

Within the Party, as Hague pointed out, membership had declined. We were not unique in this: all political parties were finding that their membership was dropping. People no longer had sufficient free time to give to organising the kind of money-raising efforts popular in the 1950s. They did not necessarily want to discuss and take part in politics as a leisure activity. With the majority of women under pension age working, they were no longer available to support Party activities as they had in the past. People were very busy with work and family. Older people were often involved in caring for grandchildren. Politics was being squeezed out of people's lives.

And there were other problems. The Party had a big overdraft, partly the result of spending £28 million on the general election, compared with the £6.7 million spent on the 1983 general election.

Our activists, though still loyal and supportive, were demoralised and inclined to blame the Parliamentary Party for sleaze, disloyalty and the 'brown envelopes' affair, which they believed had played a large part in our defeat. Our professionals – agents, Central Office workers and regional staff – were similarly demoralised, although certainly not terminally so.

It was clear that the whole Party structure would have to be recast, taking the activists, professionals and politicians with us. William Hague set out six principles by which reform would be achieved. Firstly, unity of the three component parts of the Party. Secondly, decentralisation, whereby constituency associations would henceforth be regarded as essential building blocks of the Party, with a much more direct contact between them and the Party leadership. Thirdly, democracy, through which the membership would be consulted on the manifesto and policy change. Members would also be more directly involved in the election of the leader. Fourthly, involvement, and thus a move to national membership. Fifthly, integrity, giving, through a disciplinary committee, the Party itself the power to suspend or expel. As Hague put it, the Party would not again find itself in a position 'where sustained controversy in a single constituency blackens the name of the whole Conservative Party'. And finally, openness, on Party funding.

Hague set out these proposals in July 1997, and laid out a rapid timetable for consultation on their adoption. He asked that by the end of September 1997 members should endorse his leadership and the principles of reform, and that the results of the exercise should be announced at the Party Conference that year. A Green Paper on the principles would be published before the Conference, it would be debated there and, if adopted by the Party, it would become the new constitution, to be launched at a special conference the following spring.

This exercise could only be undertaken by a party in opposition, and the amount of energy that went into it was impressive: 22,000 copies of *Blueprint for Change* were circulated; 150,000 executive summaries were sent to Party members; each constituency association was asked to complete a detailed questionnaire; twenty-six roadshows were held around the country, attended in all by 3,000 Party members; 1,200 feedback forms and letters were received from individuals, officers of associations and various Party organisations.

MPs and others rightly perceived this as a shift in power towards the activists. Many MPs had misgivings, not least because they felt that they might have to face reselection in their constituency associations. They had observed, with some anguish, the gyrations of the Labour Party when reselection was introduced. Many were the tales from Labour colleagues of the meetings and grillings they had had to endure on the road to reselection. Now Conservatives were worried that they were to face the same examination by their activists. Fears were expressed, not without foundation, that some associations would use the opportunity to force their views on to the local MP as a price for his or her reselection, with Europe, for or against, in the forefront. In the event, there were no deselections of sitting MPs. Some vengeance, however, was wreaked on those who sought to be chosen again after they had lost their seats. Many experienced great difficulty.

The endorsement of William Hague as leader and of his policies also included endorsement of his stance on Europe. He was conscious that under John Major divisions on European policy had cost the Conservative Party dear in votes and public esteem, and subsequently at the 1997 election. Meetings were held up and down the land to present the policies to members in September 1997. Returns were sent in to Central Office. These resulted in an overwhelming expression of support for William Hague as leader, and also for the policy of 'In Europe but not ruled by Europe', which he had coined. Thus, as a result of the reforms which he had introduced, and had ensured were fast-tracked, he became the first Conservative leader to have received a one member one vote endorsement from his Party membership. While this did not remove altogether a variety of opinions within the Party on the European question, it did enable the leadership to pray in aid the support they enjoyed.

The time and energy spent on modernising the Conservative Party, although of only internal importance, was an important first step in recovering from electoral defeat. It will be a lasting monument to William Hague's ability to set a course and see it through.

Hague's new team

Hague appointed his first shadow Cabinet on 20 June 1997. It combined familiar faces with new ones. Thirteen of its members had held Cabinet posts, although not all under the last government. John Redwood was brought back as shadow Trade Secretary. Norman Fowler, revived for the umpteenth time, as he himself said, became shadow Environment Secretary. Hague rang me from Yorkshire to ask if I would become shadow leader of the House. Initially I was not keen, feeling that I could do more for the Party by being out and about and not tied up in the House of Commons. However, he prevailed, and I found not only that I enjoyed the job, but also that it used some of the skills I felt I had in helping to weld together the Parliamentary Party at a potentially difficult and vulnerable time.

Newer faces included John Maples, who had been a Treasury minister before losing his seat in the 1992 election, and who became shadow Health Secretary, Francis Maude, who had also had a period out of the House, as shadow Culture Secretary, and Andrew Mackay, a former deputy Chief Whip, as shadow Northern Ireland Secretary. It was a masterstroke to make Cecil Parkinson Party Chairman. I had never worked with him but, like everyone else, soon saw that he was invaluable. Not only was he charming and self-deprecating, but he knew everyone and had seen everything before. This made his presence peculiarly comforting, and his contributions weighty. He saw the funny side of his resurrection, saying, at the Conference, that cabbage always tastes better boiled twice.

Another great source of strength was Norman Fowler. He had been in opposition before, during the Labour government from 1974 to 1979, when he had had to shadow Barbara Castle among others. He told us that no one would be interested in anything we had to say for a very long time, that we should prepare ourselves for a long haul, a year or more, before we would feel we were making headway. He also observed that in the end the shine came off all governments. How right he proved to be! Michael Heseltine, although not a member of the shadow Cabinet, and not often seen in the House, gave experienced advice when he was there. His own standing also ensured that when he chose to make a speech on any issue, it was given maximum coverage – which was not always helpful to Hague, especially with his stance on the Millennium Dome.

All the old hands understood from the start that Hague would wish eventually to have his own team, which might not include colleagues who had served in the Major Cabinets. Any new leader has the right, and indeed duty, to stamp his own authority on his inheritance. It is also self-evidently the case that, in our new situation, new people should take the Party forward, and should have their chance, as we had had. Nevertheless we were a little startled by the briefing against 'the old faces identified with the failures of the past' that appeared in the press. Several of us were picked out for special treatment – Michael Howard, Norman Fowler, John Redwood, and me. This seemed a little unjust, given that when asked to serve any of us might well have said, 'I've done my bit. Good luck, you get on with it' as many did. It was not as if it was a special pleasure to slog away in opposition after doing the job 'for real', as one colleague put it.

But my own view was that having had the privilege of office, I ought to repay my debt to the Party and to the system by serving on the frontbench at least for a period in opposition. That was why I accepted a shadow Cabinet post. I also believed that a few old hands might be useful to support William Hague in his early days as leader. It was clear that it would be an interesting challenge, but I did not feel it was my future life's work. It was irritating, therefore, to be depicted by those briefing the press as clinging to office for dear life, out of one's own grandiosity. It was even more irritating that such briefing could be taken at face value by prominent journalists, who should have known better. But the briefing had a more damaging effect than mere irritation on the part of its targets. It also allowed William Hague to be portrayed, inaccurately, as ungracious towards the colleagues with whom he had, after all, also served in the Major Cabinets and as rejecting a past of which he had been part. It was not worthy of his courage and big-heartedness. He was clearly not the source, but on one occasion the briefing was so blatant that I had it out with William, and insisted that it stop. It did, and after a month or so, I announced that I would stand down.

William handled shadow Cabinet meetings briskly and skilfully. He introduced shadow Cabinet 'Away Days' so that we could take a longer look at strategic issues, examine opinion polls and present, in a more leisurely way, policy options. A series of shadow Cabinet sub-committees was established, to look across a range of policy areas where co-ordinated approaches were required.

Renewing and modernising the Party organisation had to be achieved. William Hague, to his great credit, saw the need to do that, threw his weight and organisational capacity behind it, and achieved it in double quick time, with the support of all the disparate elements that made up the Conservative Party. He pursued this objective, the media found too dull to report, because he believed passionately that the Party should be run on democratic lines, and that it could not survive as it was. Many other leaders might have had more glamorous-seeming initial aims but Hague doggedly pushed on with reform of the Party.

Listening to Britain

In the same way, he perceived that the Party had to rid itself of the uncaring, non-listening image attached to it after eighteen years in power, so he launched 'Listening to Britain'. In the introductory document he said:

> When I became leader of the Conservative Party, I promised a fresh approach to politics. I said that Conservatives would no longer be afraid to acknowledge where we had made mistakes in the past. I recognised that, proud as we are of the achievements of the last Conservative government, the world has moved on. New problems demand fresh thinking, and new solutions. Above all, I promised that never again would we let ourselves get out of touch with the British people.

The idea was a simple one. A small unit was set up in Central Office to co-ordinate what eventually became a huge exercise. Non-Party meetings were to be set up across the country, with an independent chairman, well known locally, on specific issues, such as planning, taxation, education, transport and so on. Questionnaires would be sent out to local opinion formers before the meetings, which would be open to press and public, and views would be aired in the presence of local Conservative MPs and, if possible, a shadow spokesman. Hague took part in the first one, held in Shrewsbury, and the rest of us followed suit. I attended meetings all over the country in connection with my shadow brief, by then Environment, Transport and the Regions. I truly believed that I was not out of touch with people's preoccupations and concerns, but experience of the meetings proved me wrong. People were furious about what they perceived as the failures of the planning system, the opacity of the local government system, inaction on transport problems and, generally, about their own impotence in achieving change.

With the help of other local MPs I organised a 'Listening to Norfolk' meeting, the first, and one of only two, county-wide 'Listening to Britain' exercises. More than three hundred people attended, at the local agriculture college, on a freezing February morning. The meeting was admirably chaired by a well known local journalist, with help from the Dean of Norwich and the Director of the Rural Community Council. Despite all our efforts to make sure that the meeting was run without political bias, the local Labour Party thought otherwise, and, on the day, cobbled together a gathering for a few Labour activists, at which a hapless minister was obliged to appear, just to spoil the story, as they saw it. We saw it, and their reaction, as a success for us.

'Listening to Britain' was an overall success for the Party. Forty thousand people attended over 1,400 meetings; 250,000 responses were received to the questionnaires, consultations and other requests for information. The national media was bored by the whole exercise, but local newspapers and media gave good coverage. We all learnt a great deal. Under the same 'Listening' banner, we organised specialist meetings with health and education professionals, parents, people working in all parts of the legal system, business people, those engaged in religious activities and all faiths. The Conservative Christian Fellowship alone conducted 200 'Listening to Britain's Churches' meetings.

It was conducted alongside a programme of other policy-making activities. These included discussions conducted by frontbench teams and shadow Cabinet members. There were also high-level commissions, which so far have worked on House of Lords reform, monetary policy, the benefits of keeping the Pound, and strengthening Parliament.

Those who mock such an exercise are mistaken. The scale of the work undertaken, and the mere fact that Conservative politicians and activists sat down to listen to and discuss people's preoccupations would have been positive enough achievements. Would that we had had the time and inclination to do more of it when we were in government, and been in a position to do something about what we had learnt. But it has also meant that the policy changes we bring forward are now based on what people think needs to be done, rather than what the narrow circle of metropolitan-based opinion formers tell us should be done. It has been interesting to see the present government increasingly enmeshed with the views of the latter. When we return to government, we must ensure that we escape this form of institutionalisation.

Getting used to opposition

Being in opposition at this time has meant dealing with the special problems of our age. The accelerating pace of media communications has meant that even if policies have not been thought out, there are constant demands for an instant policy response to all government initiatives, policy changes and, of course, events. After the Conservative defeat in 1945, Winston Churchill was able to tell his colleagues that the electorate would not wish to hear from them for four years. In 1997, although we knew that that might well have been the electorate's preference, we had not the luxury of silence that our predecessors had. Nor is this a British phenomenon. My former colleague Jacques Barrot, Employment Minister in France until the election of the present Socialist government of Lionel Jospin, had found the same problem in France. And no one could accuse the French Right of inexperience in opposition.

The new Labour government plunged into frenzied activity. Every day brought fresh announcements, statements, initiatives, consultation exercises and the publication of Bills. While none of these brought great surprises, in our depleted state it was sometimes hard to keep up, and I began to understand what David Blunkett had meant as opposition education spokesman when he told me I was running him ragged with the many education initiatives I launched as Education Secretary.

Predictably the media were dazzled by all the new faces, and by the fact that the government, quite simply, were not us. They consistently ignored almost all of what we had to say on any issue, as the old hands had warned us they would. They also published tables showing how infrequently we were quoted in the press, forgetting that such mentions were in their power, not ours. Michael Fallon, one of our Treasury spokesmen, was asked to go to the Millbank studios to do an interview on why the opposition was failing to get its message across. When he arrived, he was told the interview had been cancelled. There were many new tricks to learn. One was to keep trying.

On the policy front, we had begun by thinking that we would have time to prepare policy papers, to consult widely, to take our time. We soon realised we had been wrong. While we could look forward to the duration of the Parliament before we had to prepare a manifesto, many areas required our attention immediately.

We tackled this in a number of ways. Clearly, government legislation, policy announcements, Green and White Papers could be responded to on an ad hoc basis, after shadow Cabinet discussion and agreement. Other areas, where new thinking was required, would need a different and more thorough approach.

In the past, our predecessors had used Party Backbench Committees as vehicles of policy formation when in opposition. These Committees, not to be confused with Select or All-Party Committees, shadow each department of state, have officers, and a weekly programme of meetings, visits or discussions. When I entered the Commons, election to office in the Committees was hotly contested, with different wings of the Party putting up slates. Some exercised real power and influence. An example was the Backbench Finance Committee, which was always addressed by the Chancellor of the Exchequer immediately after his Budget speech. Another was the Foreign Affairs Committee, which played a key role in the debate on Europe. In government I attached so much importance to the influence of the Committees that the Chairman of the Backbench Education Committee, James Pawsey, was an *ex-officio* member at my weekly 'prayer' meetings in the Department for Education and Employment. At MAFF, I met the backbench officers each week.

To our mild surprise – because we had thought that Backbench Committees would assume even greater importance in opposition than they had in the past – we found that attendance at and interest in the work of the Committees, with some exceptions, greatly diminished after the election. The reason for this is not hard to find, and it is a practical one: the Parliamentary Party is small, 169 MPs in all. It is quite stretching for such a relatively small number of colleagues to do all that has to be done in opposition. Attendance at Standing Committees, membership of Select Committees, work in the Chamber to keep the government on its toes, representing the Party outside the House, speaking engagements, all these normal activities for MPs take precedence over Backbench Committee work.

Scoring points

Shadow Cabinet members therefore used other means of taking forward policy development. As shadow leader of the House, a post I held for just under a year, I worked closely with constitutional experts, involving those colleagues with a natural interest, to prepare our views on strengthening Parliament, and on the constitution generally. As shadow Environment Secretary, the task was awesome. During the year I was in the post I had contact with more than 200 organisations, all with direct connections to the brief. It was important to be in touch with people who were expert in their fields and keen to talk about new policies.

The organisations ranged from the Royal Society for the Protection of Birds and Shelter, through every kind of transport lobby to the Country Landowners' Association, and all aspects of local government. I organised meetings through the Backbench Committee system every week with the aim of educating myself and my shadow team, more than from any hope that colleagues would have time to come. While all this was a strain on our administrative resources, which consisted of myself and a less than full-time secretary, we worked well together, and the shadow colleagues worked with a will to form their own connections.

It became obvious that the government would be making a policy announcement on the Right to Roam, in accordance with their manifesto commitment. We were often asked how we had found out what was going on, given that in government whole departments are devoted to setting the agenda and intelligence gathering. It was easy: some colleagues had retained contacts with the civil service, others were so involved with lobby groups that they were fully informed, while journalists, in seeking a reaction from us, naturally had to give information. We really were able to get information about anything we needed to know and, to that extent, were a little less impotent than we had expected to be.

From contacts with the National Farmers Union and the CLA, I began to piece together what the government was likely to say on the Right to Roam. At the same time, I mounted a full consultation exercise, with a questionnaire to all the relevant organisations and to colleagues in both Houses of Parliament. This culminated in a conference in Central Office, with an independent chairman, involving the Ramblers' Association, the CLA, the NFU, conservation bodies, local government interests and so on. We then produced a dossier to back up our own approach, in good time for the government's announcement.

Unusually and fortuitously, we had had adequate time for preparation in this instance: we needed a sound Party position in an area important to Conservatives. Less easy, because of the timescale, were responses to government announcements and statements in the House. The convention on these occasions is that the minister making the statement faxes through a copy about half an hour before it is due to be given in the House. When the statement is likely to be complex, much preparatory work has already gone into second-guessing its content.

This was the situation when on 20 July 1998 the government published its White Paper on Integrated Transport after many leaks and somewhat misleading press briefings. We knew from all our contacts that the White Paper had been endlessly delayed, that there had been internal disagreements about the funding and the general thrust. But we also knew, from our own experience of government, that the Treasury would be bound to hold out until the last minute, as they had done with us, and that the conservation versus motorist debate would have to have final No. 10 approval. This was the last day of the parliamentary session before the House went into its summer recess, and was chosen, no doubt, to stifle the wails from Labour backbenchers, who had been hoping to return in triumph to their constituencies, claiming their success in obtaining a new bypass or road improvement scheme. We were familiar with this kind of ploy, too, having been in that position more than once ourselves. The key point was that we were prepared, not only from the contacts we had built up with the various lobbies but from the work we had done to get our own party stance right. On the day, I was armed with all the correct questions, and all I had to do was check them with the content of the statement.

Rather different is the annual statement on the Revenue

Support Grant for local government. Local government finance is, of course, complex, and few ministers have the time while in post to grasp every last nook and cranny of it, although some, like David Curry, get close. The advantage for an opposition in preparing for this occasion is that one normally knows when it is likely to take place, around the end of November. Our own contacts in local government in turn have their own links into the department, so that by the time the statement comes the bones of it are fairly clear. Nevertheless, we put a lot of effort into getting our response right. I held a number of meetings with experts, and our own local government leaders, preparing a series of 'what if' style questions.

The day dawned. It was 2 December 1998. I had a raging cold. I had to deliver a memorial service oration at noon for the much-loved president of my constituency association, who had died the previous August. I returned to the shadow Cabinet room, where we had assembled our own Central Office number crunchers, young men of awesome application, members of our shadow team and colleagues from local government. The statement started to come through on the fax at the start of Prime Minister's Questions, which, of course, I had to miss.

I also received on my pager a message from Robert Cranborne, whom I had been going to see that night. The message said, 'Lord Cranborne regrets he is unable to dine tonight.' Shades of Miss Otis, I thought, and got on with the briefing. I had been so occupied throughout the day that I had totally missed reports of the immense row between William Hague and Lord Cranborne over the future of the House of Lords, which had come to a climax on that day.

I went up into the Chamber, clutching my questions. I also had points to make, which I was confident were relevant and awkward for the government. They were, but the Revenue Support Grant was not what was preoccupying colleagues. The Prime Minister and William Hague had just had a shouting match about the House of Lords, its future, and

Cranborne's part in it, all of which I had missed and of which I knew nothing. Our own side was agog. There was just time for someone to whisper that Blair had been having a go at William over Cranborne's behaviour, and I was on.

Hansard records that the opposition acquitted itself honourably on that occasion. I have to say that my own memory of it is hazy and of the autopilot variety. I was intensely curious to know what had happened. Whatever it was, given the whispering on our side and the stifled giggles on the other, it was serious.

After the statement, I rushed into the Tea Room for a few moments before shadow Cabinet started at 5p.m. On the way I bumped into Liam Fox, and asked him what had been going on. 'Cranborne has been negotiating direct with Blair about the future of the House of Lords, and it all came out in Prime Minister's Questions. William is furious about it. He knew nothing of it. He's in the House of Lords now,' explained Liam.

Shadow Cabinet started without William. We were told that he and the Chief Whip were in the House of Lords, meeting the Association of Conservative Peers. There had been an immense, if courteously conducted, row between him and Cranborne, before the interested gaze of the Conservative Peers. After about fifty minutes William arrived. He was clearly in a rage, bright pink, eyes shining with anger. 'I've just sacked Robert Cranborne,' he announced without ceremony. 'He has behaved duplicitously and without my knowledge or the agreement of the shadow Cabinet. So I've sacked him.' Silence followed. He then set out the sequence of events, explaining that Cranborne had put forward a plan to retain a number of hereditary peers, elected by themselves, as part of a reformed House of Lords, and until the second phase of reform was in place. This idea had been rejected by a shadow Cabinet subcommittee, but apparently Robert Cranborne had gone ahead and negotiated it direct with the government. He had had at least one meeting with the Prime Minister and with his Press Secretary. There were sharp intakes of breath around the table. No one spoke.

I decided to break the silence. I said that Robert would certainly know that he had behaved unacceptably. On the other hand, he strongly believed that his plan was supported by his colleagues, and that, in the absence of any sort of thinking from the government on the future of the House of Lords, it was the best, indeed the only way forward. I added that Cranborne had given outstanding service to the Party and to the country over many years, and we could ill afford to do without someone of his ability. At that stage my views received little support. And none of us knew then that some months later we would be told to support the deal, or something like it, when the legislation finally came before the House of Commons. Cranborne's four hundred years of experience of power would finally bear fruit.

We left the shadow Cabinet room. I need hardly have bothered with my careful preparation on the Revenue Support Grant. Never a glamorous political issue, it had dropped completely out of sight because of another great Tory row.

Parliamentary opposition parties have power and can wield it, which is always more apparent to governments than to oppositions, especially to a party newly in opposition, but it is, nevertheless, a fact. Moreover, an effective official opposition is as integral a part of a parliamentary democracy as Parliament itself. The Neill Committee, examining party political funding in October 1998, pointed out in its report that 'in a parliamentary democracy, the party in government should be held to account and kept in check by a vigorous and well-prepared opposition'.

Jennings, in *Cabinet Government*, went further, asserting that, 'if there be no opposition, there is no democracy. Her Majesty's opposition is no idle phrase. Her Majesty needs an opposition as well as a government.'

It is obvious that there is a real job for the opposition to do. By its vigour, it can focus the public's mind on important issues, can oblige the government to explain and justify itself, and can act as a conduit for public opinion on legislation. Through Parliament itself, it reminds the government of its democratic obligations. Between elections Parliament provides the vital link between the electorate and the government. The Hansard Society, in a document prepared for its own commission on the scrutiny role of Parliament, points out that 'Parliament is the principal means by which the government can be held to account for its activities.' This important and constitutional task is one of the most vital an opposition can perform.

Parliament provides the most obvious arena for the opposition. The Conservative Party had had its own parliamentary difficulties during the dying days of John Major's government. Now we had to learn new skills, against a majority of 179. Wits pointed out that quite a lot of our own MPs had had plenty of practice in opposition against their own side. Some of the best advice came from the experienced old hands, procedure men like Sir Patrick Cormack, who became the successful deputy shadow leader of the House, first to me and then to Sir George Young. Another expert was Sir Peter Emery, and yet another the formidable Nicholas Winterton, whose frequent expressions of outrage were now turned, to excellent effect, against the new government.

It was obvious to me that we needed to use all the skills available in the Parliamentary Party and to involve as many as possible in everything that was going on. We therefore established a weekly planning meeting to discuss the week's parliamentary tactics. The 1922 Committee meeting, so often either a mere formality or, when we were in government and a row was brewing, menacingly long and heavily attended, was used to present policy options or examine other longer-term issues. Progress was slow, but gradually we began to learn how to oppose.

There is no shortage of procedural opportunities for a party in opposition. One useful source is to be found in *Parliament: Functions, Practice and Procedures*, by Griffiths and Ryle, with Michael Wheeler-Booth, Clerk Assistant to the House of Lords. They produce their own version of the duties of an opposition:

> The opposition . . . must look critically at all policies and proposals brought before the House by the government and then oppose, and, if possible, delay or even prevent the implementation of those proposals it considers desirable. It will also take the initiative in seeking to bring to the public's attention aspects of the government's policies and administration which would not otherwise be brought before Parliament. And it will present its own alternative policies and proposals in the most favourable light. It will either make promises about what it would do if it came to power, or will seek to avoid making such promises in areas where it feels less secure or where its popularity might suffer.

They might have added, 'or where it thinks the government might steal them'. They go on to list the opportunities available for the opposition to question with greatest effect the policies of the government. They include the debate on the Queen's Speech, which affords the opposition leader the chance to criticise the forthcoming legislative programme in front of a full House. The same shop window is provided by the opposition leader's response to the Chancellor's Budget Statement, curiously deleted by BBC television coverage in the Budget of 2000. Some, even now, recall Margaret Thatcher's brilliance when she was replying for the opposition to the Budget in 1979. Her response was so well informed and fluent that someone called out, 'This is meant to be off the cuff,' to which she answered, 'It is a very good cuff.'

The most obvious opportunity for the opposition leader to make his or her mark is provided by Prime Minister's

Questions. That is why the present government's slick and cynical replacement of the twice-weekly slot by an over-choreographed and sycophantic photo opportunity for fawning Labour backbenchers to earn a few approval points once a week was a real blow for democratic accountability. What is immediately clear from all this is that an opposition leader ideally should be able to score in the Chamber. While it takes time for his or her superiority to be noted in the country, it rattles the government of the day, and depresses its supporters.

It is an area in which William Hague acquitted himself consistently well. Critics say it does not matter to the country at large, since people take little interest these days in the Chamber of the House of Commons. However, with the cynicism of experience, I feel that if he was not good at it, commentators would have found that it did indeed matter a great deal.

Parliamentary ambushes

Other opportunities abound. They range from set-piece debates, where a well-drilled opposition can tease out the flaws in the government's arguments, to the more opportunistic Private Notice Question, where a minister is called to the Chamber to answer a particular point of concern on a current issue, and to explain why he was apparently unwilling to offer a statement on it. The great advantage of successfully tabling a Private Notice Question is the chaos it induces in the minister's office. Almost by definition, the issue raised is one they will have been hoping to conceal. The Speaker is not obliged to give her approval or otherwise to the Question until at least midday, so all morning, the private office of the minister's department will have been in a ferment of indecision, wondering whether to cancel the day's engagements on the off-chance that the Question will have to be answered.

The media, of course, know that a Question has been put down, and the hapless minister will have to decide whether or not to accept radio and television bids. Whatever else, the issue is brought thoroughly into the open. For an opposition, it is a first-class weapon. The process in the House lasts only thirty minutes, from 3.30p.m. While the opposition will hope to shred the minister in the Chamber, the damage will already have been done. The issue has been aired, the minister's reputation for openness, and the government's, will have been questioned, the minister's day will have been ruined, and there should be positive press coverage for his tormentors.

Opposition Day debates are another useful tool to harry the government. Opposition parties are entitled to a set number of days in the parliamentary year on which they can propose the business. These are slotted into the programme, and the subjects chosen for debate are those most likely to embarrass the government, like hospital waiting lists or police numbers, where broken promises can be shown up and lavishly illustrated. Opposition Day debates afford time for preparation with the appropriate lobbies, colleagues and the press. They are most effective if they also coincide with lobbying activity on the part of the affected group, such as rural postmasters and postmistresses. A lot of effort is put in, and although the results are not always commensurate, such debates can trap ministers into making unwise promises, or unsympathetic statements, which are then usefully recorded in Hansard.

Planned and concerted attacks, against, for example, a minister under threat from his own side, or a policy where government MPs are likely to rebel, are also useful weapons for the opposition. Scalps are claimed gleefully if a minister is forced to resign after a series of unanswerable onslaughts in Parliament, backed up by unrelenting work with the press. This is an area in which John Redwood excelled, but he did not succeed by magic, rather by vigorous conviction and constant alertness.

An opposition would be unwise to measure its successes in terms of government defeats, particularly when it is pitched against one with a vast majority of 179. Some of the most effective tactics are those which cause government backbenchers to complain bitterly to their whips. Especially successful in this area has been Eric Forth, the flamboyant former education minister, with a dandyish taste in clothes and a passion for Elvis Presley. Like Dennis Skinner and Bob Cryer before him under a Conservative government, Forth has made himself an expert in procedure, and a formidable advocate for full debate of certain issues. In this he is well supported by David Maclean, an extremely able Minister of State in a number of departments before the election. They have frequently kept the House up until the small hours debating this or that point, with a clever use of procedure to ensure that they are not reprimanded by the Speaker for wasting parliamentary time.

On 25 January 2000, they executed a brilliant coup on the Disqualifications Bill by keeping the debate going throughout the night, and until 2.30p.m. the following day. The result was that the day's business was lost and with it, the Prime Minister's planned celebration, at Question Time, of his first thousand days in power. Nor was this merely a procedural matter. There were strong feelings on the opposition side about the principles at stake in the Bill, which was one of the reasons why Forth was able to summon enough speakers to keep the whole thing going. The tactic and the principles were largely ignored by the press, who did, however, manage to mention that during the night a mouse had joined the proceedings.

This kind of tactic, usually ignored as too difficult to write about by journalists, is down to internal House of Commons politics. There is a variety of opinions about the value of keeping the House up all night. Few outside know about it, and if they do, are unlikely to be impressed. But as a weapon it has the effect of raising the profile of an issue within the House, and better, of irritating the government as they trail wearily through the lobbies, not knowing when they will be allowed to go home. Nothing has got further under the skin of new Labour backbenchers than this sort of opposition activity. We wait, mischievously, for the first plaintive comments from – usually women – Labour MPs, as they wail about uncivilised hours, and family-unfriendly procedures. As these surface in the press, we know we have succeeded. Members of Parliament are regarded by the public as having a cushy life, with long holidays and no perceptible product. For them to complain about the few hours they are perceived to work does not add to their lustre, or to that of the party they represent. And the complaints inevitably give rise to suspicions that those making them do not understand the purpose of Parliament, which is not the same as that of a District Council. The attitude 'we won the election, what more do you want?' betrays a contempt for the democratic process surprising in those who never stop talking about it.

Delaying tactics are one of the opposition's few weapons. They are also important because legislative proposals may have been hastily drafted and therefore be flawed, or causing outrage in the nation. Parliament must have the time and flexibility to scrutinise what is passing before it. This was why there was some concern, and not only in the Conservative Party, when the Modernisation Committee seemed close to recommending the timetabling of all Bills. The Committee backed away from this proposal, not least because even a recently elected government with a huge majority has clear memories of its own time in opposition and the certain knowledge that it will return to it sooner or later. It would in any case be a constitutional outrage to suggest that the passage of a Bill through the parliamentary process was merely a matter of time, and rubber-stamping by a compliant House.

The House of Lords has shown the way to scrutinise legislation. It defeated the government no fewer than seventy times, between the general election and the time of its reform. Since then, it has so thoroughly scrutinised legislation passing before it that the government has been obliged to cut short various recesses and has had to timetable a large number of Bills when they have returned to the Commons. One of the results has been that the Parliamentary Labour Party, and in particular, a large number of new women MPs, are loud in their condemnation of broken promises from their own side that the conduct of House of Commons business would be made more family-friendly.

In opposition, a political party is torn between two approaches. It must undertake careful planning of policy initiatives, organisational change and thoughtful presentation of political philosophy.

But it must also take opportunistic advantage of the moment, in Parliament and through the press and media. It is no good saying you have no comment on some issue or another because you have not had time to think out your position, even if that happens to be so. The two approaches are obviously not mutually exclusive, although they sometimes come close, given the lack of manpower available. The problem diminishes as time and experience in opposition increase. At first, we discussed the need to be perceived as presenting serious alternative policies, and planning our activities, while quite frequently missing tricks. That did not last long. Apart from criticism from other quarters, our own activists were the first to point out that we should be raising the profile of this or that unpopular government policy, and we became more flexible in our responses. In the end, as systems were put into place and there was more research support, we found we could have a go at both.

Organising the opposition

Like our predecessors, we quickly ran into the problem of the resources with which to do the job. Shadow Cabinet members, in particular, found that they were required to attend conferences, make visits, keep a high profile and, of course, oppose. Many entered the shadow Cabinet with a part-time House of Commons secretary and a gap year researcher. This, of course, was just not adequate to shadow, for example, a department like Environment, Transport and the Regions, where there are ten ministers, each with a private office and press officers.

Since 1975, 'Short Money' has been available for the parliamentary work of opposition parties, named after the then leader of the House, Edward Short. The leader of the opposition and the opposition Chief Whip receive a salary. Frontbench spokesmen are entitled to some support for their work. In the past, the amount of cash each opposition party received was calculated on a formula worked out from the number of seats and votes each got in the previous general election. In 1997–98 a total of £1.5 million was made available, of which the Conservative Party received £987,000. This sum, given the important role played by opposition in our parliamentary democracy, makes an interesting contrast with the total spent by all political parties on their general election campaigns in 1997, which amounted to £56.4 million.

The whole position was investigated by the Neill Committee, and its report on the Funding of Political Parties in the United Kingdom recommended a substantial, perhaps threefold, increase in Short Money; a fixed amount for the official opposition; extra funds for the leader of the opposition; an increase in 'Cranborne' money for the work of the official opposition in the House of Lords.

The government agreed the main proposals of the Neill Report, with the result that the total amount in 1999/2000 for opposition activities is £4.8 million, of which the Conservatives receive £3.3 million.[1]

I appeared before the Neill Committee when it was deliberating and pointed out that the political process had changed out of all recognition since 1975. The Committee accepted that the raised expectations of the media, special interest groups and the inexorable rise in the amount of legislation all placed on opposition spokesmen were burdens they could not carry with the current levels of finance. It would be interesting to know if they were also influenced by the amount the Labour government was spending on political advisers, in addition to the megalithic civil service. Despite the welcome Neill increases, that development has further shifted the balance in favour of the government in defiance of the constitutional principle that both sides' activities are equally legitimate.

The role of Her Majesty's opposition

The Hansard Society Commission on the Scrutiny Role of Parliament has as its objective to examine how effectively Parliament scrutinises and holds government to account. In the document published by the Society to seek views on this matter, the following statement is made about Parliament:

> Parliament performs a number of roles in British democracy. Parliament makes the law and decides on how much the government can raise through taxation. Crucially, it also creates and sustains the government. Parliament provides the vital link between the electorate and government. Governments are accountable to the people through general elections. Between general elections, Parliament is the principal means by which the government can be held to account for its activities. This form of accountability is generally termed Parliament's scrutiny

---
1. For current levels, see previous chapter

role. Parliament performs this role by obtaining and publicising information about the government's performance and future plans. On the basis of the information, Parliament and others form a judgement as to whether the government is discharging its mandate effectively, economically and in the best interests of the electorate.

It is clearly the task of the opposition to lead this important scrutiny role. The Houghton Report on Financial Aid to Political Parties puts it thus: 'The parties in opposition have the responsibility of scrutinising and checking all the actions of the executive.'

British Government and the Constitution points out that:

> The legitimacy of opposition parties is confirmed by law, convention and the political culture of the United Kingdom. Opposition is recognised as having rights and is part of the constitutional system – as much part of it as is the government.

Ivor Jennings expands on the principle:

> Democratic government demands not only a parliamentary majority but also a parliamentary minority. The minority attacks the government because it denies the principles of its policy. The opposition will, almost certainly, be defeated in the House of Commons because it is a minority. Its appeals are to the electorate. It will, at the next election, ask the people to condemn the government, and as a consequence, to give a majority to the opposition. Because the government is criticised it has to meet criticism. Because it must in course of time defend itself in the constituencies, it must persuade public opinion to move with it. The opposition is at once the alternative to the government and a focus for the discontent of the people. Its function is almost as important as that of the government. If there be no opposition

there is no democracy. Her Majesty's opposition is no idle phrase. Her Majesty needs an opposition as well as a government.

This important statement, however, presupposes a view of the importance of Parliament, which may be becoming outdated. By how much is the power of an opposition reduced by a government that has scant regard for the parliamentary process, and by compliant media that seem to share that view? Madam Speaker's view is clear. On 5 April 2000 she reprimanded the government for yet again announcing a policy change on the *Today* programme, followed by a press conference, without informing Parliament. She said:

> It seems to me that there is a situation developing in some departments in which the interest of Parliament is regarded as secondary to media presentation, or is overlooked altogether. I hope that Ministers will set in hand a review of procedures right across Whitehall to ensure that the events that took place this morning are never allowed to happen again.

The newly elected Labour government, even before the new parliament had met, began as it meant to go on, in announcing by press conference its intention to make the Bank of England independent. The widely reported remark of Peter Mandelson in a speech in Germany in March 1998 that 'the era of pure representative democracy is coming slowly to an end' gave substance to the obvious truth that this government regarded Parliament as an outdated, slow-moving means of getting its way, and not much more. Peter Riddell commented, 'Government is becoming divorced from Parliament. For Blairites, Parliament is no longer central, it is merely one means of communication. Once in office, many ministers treat Parliament as secondary.'

The Prime Minister gave the lead in his own attitude towards Parliament. Peter Riddell revealed that Tony Blair had voted in just 5 per cent of divisions. This is in striking contrast with Margaret Thatcher's record. Even when her majority was great, in the mid-1980s, she voted in about a third of divisions. Blair lost no time after his election in announcing that he would answer Questions only once a week. For John Major and Margaret Thatcher, Questions were an important twice-weekly occasion. It is true that preparation for them took a great deal of time, but for serious parliamentarians, the constitutional necessity of answering to Parliament justified it.

Conclusion

Opposition is an important part of our parliamentary democratic process. It may be distasteful for those whose principal interest in politics is to exercise power. But for those who believe that Parliament, and its role of holding to account the government of the day on behalf of the electorate, is central to our democracy, any diminution in the power of Parliament is a threat to democracy. In the Lords debate on the report of the Royal Commission on Reform of the House of Lords, Lord Strathclyde put it this way:

> We on this side of the House do not fear a stronger Parliament. If a government carries confidence in a free, independent and respected Parliament – one not cowed by patronage or by party whips – then that government is more authoritative and respected. What destroys respect for any government is backstairs arm twisting, trading of favours, a culture of cronyism, the bypassing of Parliament and the handing of power to unelected and unaccountable advisers.

Every opposition has its own problems, born of the age in which it operates. It can and must use its time to make necessary reforms in the areas over which it has control. Its leader must unify and motivate its parliamentarians, activists and professional staff. A new opposition must have patience, be content at first with small victories, and combine careful planning with clever opportunism. Above all, through Parliament, and the media, it must restore the confidence of the public in its ability to represent their views, and hold the government to account.

3. The Corridors of (no) Power: Office Politics in the Heart of Shadow Government

Nigel Fletcher

Those who make the painful transition from government to opposition soon discover that when you lose office in Britain, you do so quite literally. As well as Downing Street itself, there are dozens of government departments and agencies, all housed in vast buildings and employing thousands of civil servants. It all amounts to a lot of office space and staff support that is lost overnight following an election defeat.

Whereas a party entering government finds a fully resourced and staffed Whitehall empire waiting to house them, a party making the reverse journey finds itself virtually homeless and unsupported. They have their party headquarters and staff, albeit exhausted and hugely scaled down following the election campaign, but for their duties as the official opposition, outgoing governments have in recent times found themselves restricted to a small suite of offices in the House of Commons, and limited personal staff to cope with the huge upheaval.

For these reasons, life is chaotic for the newly powerless, as Gillian Shephard's account in the previous chapter confirms. John Major noted that in the first days after the 1997 election 'with No. 10 now occupied by Tony Blair and parliament in recess, I did not even have an office from which to work'. Mounds of correspondence were delivered directly to his private home, and those trying to reach the former Prime Minister by phone, including former US President George Bush Snr, were greeted by a domestic answering machine.

On moving into the leader of the opposition's offices in the Commons, he describes them, rather generously, as 'ill-equipped'.[1]

Likewise, when Labour left office in 2010, the change must have been disorientating for those who had only known government. The contrast between the grand, iconic and very public nature of 10 Downing Street and the largely unknown, shabby and hidden rooms into which ex-ministers filed for their first shadow Cabinet meeting would have been stark. But they were also following in the distinguished footsteps of many previous shadow ministers who have met in such rooms and eventually gone on to enjoy the fruits of office. If an opposition is a government-in-waiting, their offices are the most significant waiting-rooms in Britain.

The history of these rooms and their occupants is rarely told, but what follows hopefully places the challenges of being in opposition in their physical context.

Clement Attlee: 1935–40

By 1937, when Clement Attlee became the first leader of the opposition to receive an extra salary for his duties, there had long been a room set aside in the Commons specifically for the holder of the post. At the time, with office space in Parliament at a premium, the working methods of Labour's leadership were by necessity close-knit. Attlee recalled that from 1931, his predecessor as Labour leader, George Lansbury, 'invited [Stafford] Cripps and me to share with him the leader of the opposition's room at the House and the three of us worked together in great harmony'.[2]

Attlee occupied this room first as deputy leader, then as leader from 1935, retaining its use throughout the five years he served in the wartime coalition government, and only moving

---
1. *John Major – the Autobiography* (HarperCollins, 1999)
2. *As it Happened*, Clement Attlee (Windmill Press, 1954)

out when he became Prime Minister in 1945.[3] During his time as leader of the opposition, this room would have been a hub of activity, with the Executive Committee (shadow Cabinet) meeting for an hour every day before Questions.[4]

Winston Churchill: 1945–51

Following Attlee's move to No. 10, the defeated Winston Churchill took over the same room, although he spent rather less time in it than his predecessor. He was an infrequent attendee at the House of Commons during this period, and did not always trouble himself unduly with the views of his shadow Cabinet colleagues, a fact which has often been cited as a key weakness in his approach to opposition.[5] He was also frequently absent abroad, leaving Anthony Eden to shoulder the burden on his behalf.

When he was in town, Churchill spent a lot of his time working at his London home, 28 Hyde Park Gate. He employed three secretaries there, and acquired the house next door to provide extra space for them. His correspondence as leader was sent not on House of Commons stationery, but on paper headed with his London address or that of his beloved country retreat of Chartwell in Kent.[6]

If the centre of influence in opposition is the vicinity of its leader, the House of Commons at this time had to compete with Hyde Park Gate, Chartwell, and the Savoy Hotel, where Churchill would periodically move meetings of the shadow Cabinet, over a good lunch.[7]

Given the importance of domestic settings to Churchill's working patterns, it is perhaps appropriate that around this

---
3. Ibid. p. 214
4. Ibid.
5. *The Conservative Party in Opposition*, J. D. Hoffman (Macgibbon & Kee, 1964)
6. E.g. Churchill to Attlee, 6 October, 10 October & 27 October 1946 (PREM 8/309 210595)
7. *Churchill*, Roy Jenkins (Pan Books, 2002)

time the issue of the leader of the opposition's accommodation had entered onto the agenda of government. In February 1951, an official in the Lord Chancellor's office wrote to a counterpart in No. 10 about an offer from a generous benefactor, one Colonel Medcalf, who 'would like to present his house as a residence for the official leader of the opposition', along with an endowment to pay for its upkeep.[8] No. 10 passed the matter to the Treasury, where officials considered the merits of accepting the offer.

The building, an eighteenth-century red brick house called Capel Manor, was located in Enfield, north London, and had been offered originally by Colonel Medcalf to the National Trust, who had turned it down as unworthy of preservation.[9] The Treasury also seemed less than convinced, with an official there pondering: 'The question is simply whether we want a house for the purpose suggested. That is, I suppose, outside my scope. If it is a fine democratic thing to give the leader of the opposition an official salary, I suppose it might be equally admirable to give him a house; but that argument could be carried in all directions.'[10] Having thus considered the matter, he concluded: 'My general feeling is that the leader of the opposition seems to be getting along quite well without an official house.'[11]

The senior Treasury official to whom this memo was addressed (the Dickensian-sounding Mr Playfair), concurred with this view, adding 'It is doubtful whether it is a suitable idea to have an official residence for the leader of the opposition, and we do not really need, or want, more official residences

---

8. Letter from W. T. C. Skyrme, Lord Chancellor's Office, to E. G. Cass, Downing Street, 13 February 1951 (National Archives T 219/211).
9. Letter from J. F. W. Rathbone, National Trust, to Colonal Medcalf, 17 October 1950 (T 219/211)
10. Memo from unknown official to Mr Playfair, Treasury, 22 February 1951 (T 219/211)
11. Ibid.

for Ministers.'[12] Colonel Medcalf's offer was politely declined, and Capel Manor eventually became an agricultural college.

It is not recorded whether Winston Churchill as leader of the opposition was ever consulted over the offer, but given his love of Chartwell, it seems fair to say he was 'getting along quite well' without another house. His successor, Clement Attlee, may have had a rather different view. When Labour lost office in October 1951 Attlee recorded that moving from Downing Street was 'a considerable business' because of the large number of possessions, including caskets containing the Charters of Freedom of several cities, which now 'had to find their places in a small house'. This issue of eviction of former prime ministers was to arise again later.

Back at Westminster, Attlee reoccupied his old office once more, but had to get used to commuting into London every day from his house in Prestwood, after eleven years in Downing Street. In adapting to life out of office he records his good fortune in securing the services of a 'first-class' secretary, Mrs Skelly, whilst Arthur Moyle continued as his parliamentary Private Secretary.[13]

Growing pains

When Hugh Gaitskell moved into the leader of the opposition's room after Attlee's retirement, problems of lack of space began to make life difficult. In 1960, action to address the issue was proposed.

The Chairman of the Speaker's Committee on Accommodation, Sir James Duncan, told his colleagues at a meeting around July 1960 that the leader of the opposition's secretaries' room was 'woefully inadequate' given it had to accommodate 'two secretaries and all their paraphernalia as

---
12. Letter from E. W. Playfair to Sir Eric de Norman, Minister of Works, 28 February 1951 (T 219/211)
13. *As it Happened*, Clement Attlee (Windmill Press, 1954), p. 214

well as a parliamentary Private Secretary'.[14] He proposed that some of the waiting space outside the room be incorporated into it by moving the wall further out into the corridor. It was not considered feasible to reduce the size of Mr Gaitskell's own office, as this was already 'barely large enough to take meetings of the shadow Cabinet'.[15]

After consultation with the surveyor of the Houses of Parliament, a minute was prepared for the Minister setting out the feasibility of the scheme. This highlighted the difficulties of making alterations to this sensitive part of the Palace of Westminster, the minimal space that would be created, and the relatively high cost of £600 for the works. It also mentions an alternative scheme put forward by the surveyor to avoid such a necessity. The leader of the opposition's office was then situated next to that of the leader of the House of Commons, and it was suggested Gaitskell could swap with his neighbour Rab Butler, whose secretaries' room was larger.

The Ministry of Works concluded that this alternative was not practical, since Butler's own room was smaller than Gaitskell's, which had already been acknowledged as barely adequate. The decision was therefore made to go ahead with the original plan, and work was completed by the end of October.[16]

'The key': Harold Wilson 1963–64

When Harold Wilson took over as leader following Gaitskell's untimely death, the continuing practical constraints of working from the House of Commons quickly became apparent. This led to a saga that devotees of *Yes Prime Minister* will find sounds somewhat familiar. In July 1963, Wilson wrote to

---
14. Memorandum from A. W. Cunliffe, Ministry of Works, 22 July 1960 (WORK 11/657)
15. Ibid.
16. Memorandum from A. W. Cunliffe, Ministry of Works, to Minister, 16 August 1960 (WORK 11/ 657)

the Serjeant at Arms, asking if there was any reason why his secretary, the notorious Marcia Williams, could not use his office on a Saturday, as she had apparently been told by an attendant that she could not. The Serjeant assured Wilson this was not the case, and the attendant had been misinformed.[17]

Mrs Williams continued to experience difficulties, however, and several heated rows ensued. A particularly explosive encounter occurred on Saturday 20 July when a 'custodian' of the House tried to tell her the room was to be kept locked at weekends, and she would have to find one of his colleagues to let her in, and report back when she had finished in the room. At this, the unfortunate attendant reported, 'she got on her high horse' and asked 'what, me in my position?' Another custodian arriving on the scene fared little better, as 'she started shouting at him, too'.[18]

The fall-out from this incident led to the Lord Great Chamberlain (who had overall responsibility for the Palace of Westminster at the time) writing to Wilson to apologise, but defending the necessity of the room being locked. He also noted that Williams had put the custodians in some difficulty by 'bringing in a stranger without prior warning', a reference to an assistant secretary.[19] Wilson retorted that this was likely to happen from time to time, given 'the amount of work in my office is so heavy that my secretary often needs extra help'. With regard to his office, he said, 'If it is now always to be locked at the weekend, I think I must have a key for myself – as is the case with even junior Ministers – since I very often want to pop in on Saturdays.'[20]

His request was not fully met, although a compromise was reached with the addition of an extra Yale lock, to which Wilson was given two keys. But problems still persisted with access during the parliamentary recess. In the end, the

17. Serjeant at Arms' memo and papers, July 1963 (HL/BR/2/259)
18. Memo from Custodian Hall, House of Lords, 22 July 1963 (HL/BR/2/259)
19. Letter from Lord Great Chamberlain to Harold Wilson, 24 July 1963 (HL/BR/2/259)
20. Letter from Wilson to Lord Great Chamberlain, 25 July 1963 (HL/BR/2/259)

authorities conceded the best plan would be for Wilson's rooms to be left unlocked at the end of the early morning cleaning period as it was in daily use during recess.[21] But it seems he never got his key.

Edward Heath: 1965–70

When he became leader in 1965, Edward Heath took a rather unorthodox approach to getting stuck into the job – he went on holiday to the south of France. This, he later conceded, was not wise, and left him besieged by press and a mass of congratulatory letters, which, having no secretary with him, he attempted to answer by hand, leaving him 'more tired at the end of the holiday than at the beginning'.[22]

When he returned, Heath appointed John MacGregor as his Private Secretary and head of his office. He appreciated MacGregor's Scottish roots as a means of keeping him well briefed on Scottish matters, and prided himself on spending more time in Scotland than any of his predecessors or successors. The closeness of the office arrangements were emphasised when MacGregor later married Jean Dungey, one of Heath's secretaries.[23] In 1966 Douglas Hurd joined the team, although his exact position was not clear. Heath's memoirs state he was appointed as 'political secretary',[24] but Hurd's own recollection is somewhat different. He left the Diplomatic Service to join the Conservative Research Department as a foreign affairs adviser, after writing to Edward Heath and being referred to Sir Michael Fraser, the then head of the Department. Although Fraser had implied to him he would be part of Ted Heath's team, this was never spelled out. Hurd recalled this ambiguity caused

---
21. Letter from Lord Great Chaimberlain to Harold Wilson, 3 September 1963 (HL/BR/2/259)
22. *The Course of my Life*, Edward Heath (Hodder and Stoughton, 1998)
23. Ibid.
24. Ibid.

embarrassment when, unlike his superiors in the CRD, he was invited to meetings with Heath in his apartment at Albany. It soon became clear, Hurd notes, 'that Ted regarded us as his inner Cabinet in continental style.'[25] Alongside John MacGregor, the gatherings also included Heath's speechwriter Michael Wolff and the young economist Brian Reading.

John MacGregor left running the leader's office in 1968, and was succeeded by Douglas Hurd, who was offered the job by Heath's parliamentary Private Secretary, Jim Prior, who according to Hurd 'exercised more influence on Ted at this time than any other individual.'[26] On taking over, Hurd found the workload daunting, and began looking for an 'adjutant' to take over routine administration. After initially considering the young Jeffrey Archer for the post, Hurd eventually settled on Cyril Townsend, who 'did the job admirably' and later became MP for Bexleyheath.[27]

During this time, much activity continued to be focused on his office in the House of Commons, where the shadow Cabinet met weekly, usually on a Wednesday.[28] Despite the alteration made for Gaitskell, the facilities were still not considered spacious. Douglas Hurd recalls that the work of handling correspondence, managing Heath's diary and organising shadow Cabinet meetings was undertaken by a small team 'squashed into a small anteroom to a House of Commons office'. As well as this formal base at the Commons, Heath continued to hold irregular meetings of his advisers at Albany. It was here that they met to plan the Selsdon Park Hotel Conference at which the shadow Cabinet finalised the 1970 manifesto.[29]

---

25. *Memoirs – Douglas Hurd* (Little, Brown, 2003)
26. Ibid.
27. Ibid.
28. *The Path to Power*, Thatcher (HarperCollins, 1995)
29. *Memoirs – Douglas Hurd* (Little, Brown, 2003)

Harold Wilson: 1970–74

When Wilson returned to opposition following Heath's victory, the inconveniences were exacerbated by the unexpectedness of the result. He had no home to go to, and after enjoying the courtesy extended to ex-prime ministers of a final weekend at Chequers, he moved first to a flat in Westminster belonging to a wealthy industrialist, before finding a temporary house to rent in Vincent Square.[30]

There was also a problem with moving into the opposition's offices in the House of Commons, as Edward Heath's staff sought initially to retain possession until the following Monday. This was thwarted by a typically robust response from Marcia Williams, who demanded their immediate eviction. This would have occurred, except for the attitude of the Ministry of Works porters tasked with moving Heath's effects, who were so upset by Labour's defeat that they refused to lift a finger to help the Conservatives.[31] They were eventually persuaded by the provision of some bottles of beer, but took so long that there was no time left to help Wilson's staff clear many of their belongings from No. 10, and these had to be left in a basement of Downing Street awaiting removal over the weekend.[32]

Over at the House of Commons, another petty squabble arose over Wilson's television set, which had been moved from the Prime Minister's room to the leader of the opposition's. House authorities insisted it should be left for Heath's use, and moved it back, despite the fact Wilson had paid for it himself. It took the intervention of a No. 10 official before the dispute was resolved in Wilson's favour.[33]

Marcia Williams recalls that, the television aside, the leader's room had changed little since she had occupied it over five years before: 'The room looked just the same. The

---
30. *Glimmers of Twilight*, Joe Haines (Politico's, 2003), p. 32
31. Haines (2003), p. 31
32. *Inside Number 10*, Marcia Williams (Weidenfeld and Nicholson, 1972), p. 18
33. Ibid.

furniture was arranged in the same way. Even the dust seemed familiar. It was hard, too, not to recall the old feeling of our office routine five and a half years before.'[34] This office routine got off to a shaky start, however. On his first day back, Wilson decided to summon a meeting of his old Cabinet, who would stand in until the Parliamentary Labour Party could, in accordance with its rules, elect a shadow Cabinet. He asked his close aide Joe Haines for their phone numbers, but encountered a problem. Haines recalls: 'I didn't have all of them. With the Downing Street switchboard available, Wilson hadn't had to dial a phone number since 1964. With some help from the Parliamentary Labour Party office, we compiled a list and he set about calling each of them.'[35]

On 29 June 1970, eleven days after his defeat at the hands of the electorate, Harold Wilson was re-elected leader of the Labour Party and was thus leader of the opposition once more, just in time to take his place at the Despatch Box for the Queen's Speech debate on the 2 July. Nine days later Roy Jenkins was elected deputy leader, beating both Fred Peart and Michael Foot, whilst Bob Mellish was also confirmed as Chief Whip. The elections for the shadow Cabinet (officially the Parliamentary Committee) took place on the 16 July, with nine of the twelve MPs elected being members of the previous Cabinet.[36]

The new shadow Cabinet met for the first time that same day, and the experience was described in less than impressed terms by Michael Foot, who wrote: 'The whole discussion proceeded in a most disorderly manner, much less formal . . . than meetings of the Tribune Group. One had to elbow one's way into the discussion.' He also noted that the proceedings were 'at moments slightly raucous or comic', that Harold Wilson 'seemed to carry little authority', before concluding

---
34. Ibid.
35. Haines (2003), p. 33
36. Patrick Bell, *The Labour Party in Opposition 1970–74* (Routledge, 2004)

that membership of the shadow Cabinet 'will take years off my life and theirs'.[37] This last prediction was unfounded, at least in his own case, and he lived for another forty years to the ripe old age of ninety-six.

The stress of defeat seems to have added to the tensions that existed amongst Wilson's staff at the time, particularly that between Marcia Williams and Joe Haines, his Press Secretary. Haines has recorded that it was only after they entered opposition and were working more closely together than in government that their relationship began seriously to break down. Initially, Williams announced she would confine her work to being Wilson's Private Secretary, leaving Haines to be the de facto office manager. He recalls 'I immediately started to plan the reorganisation (or, more strictly, the organisation, for there was none) of the office. We had nine secretaries, far too many for opposition and hopelessly beyond the ability of either Wilson or the party to pay for them.'[38] But before he could proceed further, he discovered that Williams had already reneged on their agreement, and posted up a rota for the secretaries, with their exact duties and responsibilities assigned. Her overbearing manner extended to banning the secretaries from making tea in their office, rather unfairly, given the nearest cafeteria was some distance away. Such behaviour led directly to at least one of the secretaries resigning from the leader's office.[39]

From Haines' account, and what we know of the layout of the offices at that point, it seems that Williams and her immediate assistants occupied the secretaries' room immediately outside the leader's office, whilst other secretaries, and presumably Haines himself, were based in rooms on the floor above.

It did not take long for the lack of resources in opposition to make themselves apparent again. At a meeting of the shadow

---
37. Ibid.
38. Haines (2003), p. 34
39. Ibid.

Cabinet on 11 November that year, Anthony Crosland raised the issue of research assistance to shadow ministers, and put forward three options for consideration – assistance from Labour Party HQ (which he thought unlikely), raising private finance, or by somehow creating 'a department of the opposition'. The prospect of receiving support from the Party receded as it became apparent that Labour was severely in debt. Wilson himself was able to staff his own office only by accepting financial backing from business people, not all of them entirely respectable, and from the proceeds of his publishing deal for writing an account of his administration.

Edward Heath: 1974–75

The rather brutal manner in which defeated prime ministers are ejected from office resulted in Edward Heath, as Harold Wilson before him, having no accommodation to move into. This prompted the matter of accommodation for the leader of the opposition to be raised once again. During the debate on the Queen's Speech in 1974 following the general election, Jeremy Thorpe intervened to say:

> What is quite outrageous – and I do not intend embarrassing any individual, but this must be said – is the way in which we bundle prime ministers out of their residence rather as if the bailiff had arrived for non-payment of rent without even a county court hearing. . . This is not the way that a person who has held a position of great responsibility should be treated.[40]

He felt it should be possible for the government to have a house which could be used for government hospitality between elections, then used if needed by an outgoing prime minister. Having been given notice of the question, Harold Wilson replied that he was 'only too conscious of this

40. Hansard, 12 March 1974, col. 86

problem', and that he had started discussions on the subject that morning. His deliberations are recorded in a Downing Street memorandum entitled 'Residence for the Leader of the Opposition' which show that discussions took place on the possibility of buying a town house within reach of the House of Commons for the purpose.

Whitehall was noticeably lukewarm, with one civil servant noting that it would be difficult to justify providing such a facility at the taxpayers' expense, and that the reason cited by Thorpe of providing somewhere for an outgoing prime minister to stay after losing office was not compelling. The defeated PM would have at least some inclination that sudden eviction from No. 10 were a possibility, and it was difficult to conceive that they would be left entirely homeless. As, the official noted cattily, 'Even Mr Heath has friends.'[41]

This may have been the case, but it soon became clear he did not have enough friends within the Parliamentary Conservative Party to sustain his leadership, and in early 1975 he was 'bundled out', to be replaced by Margaret Thatcher.

Margaret Thatcher: 1975–79

When Mrs Thatcher took over as leader of the opposition, her private office was headed by her close confidant Airey Neave, who had played a leading role in her leadership election campaign and whom she also appointed shadow Northern Ireland Secretary. The day after the leadership election Thatcher met with the secretaries who had worked for Heath, and recalls 'They were clearly upset, and I detected some hostility. This was quite understandable; indeed, I thought it a tribute to their loyalty.'[42] She asked them to stay on if they felt able, and most of them did so, at least for a time.

---

41. Letter from Civil Service Department to Property Services Agency, 19 March 1974 (T341/854)
42. *The Path to Power*, Margaret Thatcher (HarperCollins, 1995), p. 293

As far as office space was concerned, she was far from impressed by the facilities. She recalls there 'was not enough space, and as summer approached it all became very hot and airless'.[43] The limitations of the facilities were underlined by the fact her secretaries had to sit on the floor in the main room to sort the huge pile of correspondence she received.[44]

The volume of mail was the first test of the office organisation, with staff coming across from Central Office to help sort it, but most of the effort falling to the four secretaries, who Thatcher recalls 'did their best, but it was hopelessly unsystematic'. After a while, and at the suggestion of Party Treasurer Alistair McAlpine, she appointed David Wolfson, the man responsible for the mail-order section of Great Universal Stores, to take charge of the correspondence section and bring some order to the chaos.[45]

She also attempted to make her surroundings bearable, to limited effect, as a journalist who interviewed her there in May 1975 reported: 'Margaret Thatcher has persuaded the Department of the Environment to embellish the leader of the opposition's room with a couple of cloth-covered settees and an armchair, a pink-shaded brass lamp and a chromium and glass table. There should be some impressionist prints coming. The plates on the mantel-piece are her own. Only half the bulbs in the chandelier light up, which has her snapping switches in mild exasperation.'[46]

Her office routine made the inadequacies of the office more troublesome. In the same interview she revealed that she was normally in her office by 9.30a.m. and stayed at least until the House of Commons rose for the night, frequently much later: 'By the time I've been writing a speech at three o'clock in the morning, my hair is looking dishevelled. I haven't even got a mirror in this room, I must get one. You look in the glass of

---

43. *The Path to Power*, Margaret Thatcher (HarperCollins, 1995), p. 293
44. *The Path to Power*, Margaret Thatcher (HarperCollins, 1995)
45. Ibid.
46. Brian Connell, *The Times*, 19 May 1975

the bookcase or something, but you make up before you go out in the morning, you put on something reasonably tidy and you hope it remains reasonably tidy.'[47]

Alongside Airey Neave (who had other demands on his time as a result of his parliamentary responsibilities) Mrs Thatcher appointed a full-time head of her office, Richard Ryder, who was at the time working on the *Daily Telegraph*'s gossip column 'Peterborough' and was recommended by the paper's editor, Bill Deedes, an old friend of Thatcher's. Ryder, she recalled, ran the small office 'very effectively on a shoe-string' and it was 'a happy ship'. So much so that Ryder followed the example set by John MacGregor and eventually married Caroline Stephens – one of the secretaries inherited from Ted Heath.[48]

A month after Ryder's arrival, the former TV producer Gordon Reece came on secondment from EMI for a year, to help with managing the press, 'and much else' as Thatcher puts it. In her words he was 'a Godsend' and his impact went far beyond his formal responsibilities, extending to arranging vital media training and a makeover of the inexperienced leader's wardrobe, appearance and, famously, her voice.[49]

The by-now familiar pressures of lack of space had been a concern to Mrs Thatcher's staff from the time she became leader. It was raised with the government, and for a time there was a proposal for the opposition to take over No. 1 Abbey Gardens, near Parliament, but this was ruled out on g rounds of cost. Then at the beginning of May 1976, Airey Neave approached the new leader of the House, Michael Foot, to ask if there was any possibility of the opposition taking over some of the accommodation in the Serjeant at Arms' official residence, off Speaker's Court in the Palace of Westminster.[50] With approval finally given by the Prime Minister, Mrs

---
47. Ibid.
48. Ibid.
49. *The Path to Power*, Margaret Thatcher (HarperCollins, 1995), p. 297
50. Minute from C. H. Saville, Lord President's Office, to M. W. Townley, Cabinet Office, 6 May 1976 (HL PWO/11/23)

Thatcher vacated her old rooms by September. These were made available for Cabinet ministers. The former leader's room became the Home Secretary's office, and remains as such today. As for the new premises, Neave was at pains to stress the lack of work needed or desired in the new billet. Thatcher agreed: the careful display of frugality demonstrates the sensitivity of a politician aware of the potential dangers of extravagance at a time of national restraint, as well, perhaps, as Mrs Thatcher's own instincts on good housekeeping.

The new suite contained a room for the leader, facing New Palace Yard, with adjoining offices for staff partially located within the base of the Clock Tower. There was also the shadow Cabinet's new meeting room in the Serjeant's old dining room, facing out onto Speaker's Green and Westminster Bridge. Next to this was a wood-panelled anteroom which had formerly served as the Serjeant's study. Mrs Thatcher's insistence on restraint in the redecoration was vindicated when Labour MP Dennis Skinner put down a parliamentary question the following month asking about the costs.[51] The answer from the Minister at the Department for the Environment was a succinct 'about £900', but the background note provided by civil servants gives additional evidence of the frugality of the exercise, stressing 'it was a special request of the leader of the opposition that nothing should be purchased for her new accommodation at the House and no major redecoration work carried out'.

From these offices, Mrs Thatcher held court for the duration of her period as leader. She recalls that she not only worked, but also entertained there during the week when the House was sitting, receiving visitors including Ronald Reagan, who came to see her there whilst still a presidential hopeful in November 1978.[52] She certainly made herself at home, as one of her staff recalled. Matthew Parris, who

---
51. Parliamentary Question, DOE 5192/75/76, 19 October 1976 (HL PWO/11/23)
52. *The Path to Power*, Margaret Thatcher (HarperCollins, 1995) p. 309

worked in her correspondence unit, recalls an occasion just before a shadow Cabinet meeting when he walked into the shadow Cabinet room to find the leader of Her Majesty's Loyal Opposition standing on a wobbling chair in stockinged feet, running her finger along the top of an oil painting. 'It's the way a *woman* knows whether a room's been cleaned *properly*,' she told him.[53]

Mr Parris's own view of the leader's office was less homely. He recorded that 'though there were many rooms, the impression lent by the fevered braggadocio of Barry's and Pugin's hateful, overheated neo-Gothic monstrosity, the Palace of Westminster, was of cramp and conspiracy'.[54]

Labour in opposition: 1979–92

Labour's long years in opposition began with former Prime Minister James Callaghan serving as leader of the opposition for a year before standing down to be replaced by Michael Foot, who had earlier played such a crucial role in transferring the shadow Cabinet room to the opposition's use. For three years he chaired meetings there, many of which saw violent internal disputes, often involving Tony Benn, who took copious notes during meetings, much to the annoyance of his colleagues.

When he became leader in 1983, Neil Kinnock put together a private office of trusted aides, headed by his executive assistant Richard (Dick) Clements, a friend of his since the early 1970s, who had left his post as editor of *Tribune* the previous year to head Michael Foot's office. The rest of the young team contained a number of people who were to play a major role in Labour politics in the future. As his personal assistant Kinnock appointed Charles Clarke, who had been his research assistant in Parliament since 1981. He took responsibility for day-to-day administration, leaving Clements to concentrate on links

---
53. *Chance Witness*, Matthew Parris (Penguin, 2003)
54. Ibid.

with the Parliamentary Labour Party, shadow Cabinet and trade unions. This division was formalised when Clarke took the title of Chief of Staff eighteen months later.[55]

Patricia Hewitt, former General Secretary of the National Campaign for Civil Liberties, was appointed Press Secretary, whilst political research was assigned to John Reid, who joined after working for the Scottish Union of Students, and would later become Home Secretary under Tony Blair. He worked in the cramped outer office in the base of the Big Ben tower.

Kinnock's private office attracted criticism from within the Party for its size (being larger than Michael Foot's), and for its youth. Some Labour MPs are reported to have described them as the 'Sixth form' and 'Kindergarten Cabinet', with one commenting that 'It's not the National Union of Students we're asking him to run.'[56] The new team introduced a more formalised regime, with Patricia Hewitt making clear to journalists that all media contacts would go through her, not directly to her boss.[57]

Meanwhile, MPs and shadow ministers, including deputy leader Roy Hattersley, began to get frustrated with having to make an appointment to meet Kinnock, rather than being able to wander into the leader's office as they could when Michael Foot was there. All appointments had to be arranged through the 'formidably efficient' Sue Nye (diary secretary), and space was seldom found.[58] The more regulated approach to the diary was summarised in a memo from Charles Clarke to Kinnock which stated firmly: 'This means saying "No" to pressing MPs. . . You must never depart from the principle that you will never make a commitment to anybody for your diary, and that the office decision is final.'[59]

---

55. *Kinnock: The Biography*, Martin Westlake (Little, Brown, 2001)
56. Ibid.
57. Ibid.
58. Ibid.
59. Charles Clarke, 'Analysis of 1984 speeches', Kinnock Collection Box 252, cited in *Kinnock – The Biography*, Martin Westlake (Little, Brown, 2001)

There were some elements of informality remaining. He continued to hold weekly off-the-record press briefings, and the atmosphere at these was recorded by BBC reporter Nicholas Jones:

> Journalists remembered with affection the mateyness of the sessions that took place late each Thursday afternoon, when they would assemble in the shadow Cabinet room. At the appointed hour Kinnock would breeze in. Out would come his pipe and tobacco... It was a moment to be savoured: the union banners hanging on the wood-panelled walls, the Welsh accent and the fragrance of the pipe smoke conjured up a rich political history.[60]

With the Labour Party at this time containing a bewildering mix of joint committees of various interest groups, the opposition's offices played host to more than just the leader and shadow Cabinet. In November 1983, a month after his election, Kinnock chaired the first meeting of the Campaign Strategy Committee, consisting of twenty-three members, including representatives from the Labour Party National Executive Committee, the Parliamentary Labour Party, four trade unions and the Labour MEPs.

The room also provided the backdrop for the final scene in Kinnock's leadership. Just before the general election of 1992, the House of Commons authorities discussed with the opposition the replacement of the curtains in the shadow Cabinet room, and Kinnock's office decided on gold, having allegedly been asked to change the existing colour, red, to avoid any embarrassment if the Conservatives moved in after polling day.[61] When this consideration became irrelevant and Kinnock resigned the leadership, he chose the shadow Cabinet room for his valedictory statement, flanked by his wife and closest personal staff, with a South Wales area

---

60. *Soundbites and Spin Doctors*, Nicholas Jones (Indigo Books, 1996)
61. *Sunday Times*, 12 January 1992

National Union of Mineworkers banner and a display of red roses behind him.[62]

John Smith: 1992–94

When he became leader, John Smith signalled a clear change in style, replacing the banner on the wall with a painting showing 'a rainswept Palace of Westminster across a grey, storm-tossed Thames'.[63] He also moved his base from the existing opposition rooms on the principal floor of the Commons to a larger office upstairs, where he had room for a conference table and a sofa.[64]

As his Chief of Staff, Smith appointed Murray Elder, who had previously been General Secretary of the Scottish Labour Party, and a long-term ally of Smith. His aim, it was noted at the time, was to bring together the three power bases of the Labour Party – the Walworth Road Party HQ, the Parliamentary Party, and the leader's office.[65]

The period between the death of John Smith and the election of Tony Blair to replace him has been perhaps the most documented – and disputed – leadership transition in modern times. But once the controversy of the events leading up to the 'Granita' deal with Gordon Brown was over, and Blair's leadership campaign was officially launched, the shape of the team which was to serve him in opposition and through to government began to emerge. Robin Cook turned down the offer of becoming campaign manager, and the job went instead to Jack Straw and Mo Mowlam. Meanwhile, friends Barry Cox and Michael Levy took on the role of fundraisers, whilst Peter Mandelson continued to give advice behind the

---

62. *The Times*, 14 April 1992
63. *Sunday Times*, 6 December 1992
64. *If John Smith had lived*, Channel 4, 1999
65. 'Smith aides seek to ensure unity at the top', *Financial Times*, 20 July 1992

scenes, against the wishes of the official team, and without the knowledge of many of them.[66]

Meanwhile, the formal role of leader of the opposition had to be filled, and Labour's deputy leader Margaret Beckett became acting leader until the conclusion of the election process. She inherited Smith's staff, government car, and the formal duties that went with the job such as Prime Minister's Questions and meeting foreign dignitaries. She brought a certain informality to the job, with her husband Leo acting as her assistant, once being seen by a journalist poking his head around the door of the shadow Cabinet room to ensure he knew where his wife was should a foreign head of government call.[67]

Tony Blair: 1994–97

Since entering Parliament, Tony Blair had existed with a small staff, centred since 1987 around his long-time friend and confidante Anji Hunter. But on becoming leader, he decided to establish a much larger and more professional operation which would assist with the anticipated transition to government.[68] It was a daunting challenge – Blair later remarked to Iain Duncan Smith that going from being leader of the opposition to Prime Minister is 'nothing like the jump you take from being a member of the shadow Cabinet into being leader of the opposition'.[69]

This required extra resources, and Michael (later Lord) Levy continued his campaign role in helping raise the funds to pay for it. Anji Hunter took on the role of head of the private office, and whilst many of the staff from Smith's

---

66. *Blair*, Anthony Seldon (Free Press, 2005)
67. The *Independent on Sunday*, 26 June 1994
68. *Blair*, Anthony Seldon (Free Press, 2005)
69. Interview with Iain Duncan Smith, 10 December 2003: Committee on Standards and Privileges, Fourth Report of Session 2003–04 (HC 476–III, House of Commons, 29 March 2004)

private office did not have their contracts renewed, Murray Elder, as a close confidant of the late leader, initially stayed on to work on trade union relations, before leaving to become a lobbyist in January 1995. Alastair Campbell became Press Secretary, assisted by Hilary Coffman, who had worked for both Kinnock and Smith, Tim Allen, who had already worked for Blair, and Peter Hyman, who took over speech-writing duties.[70]

Blair moved his office back to the principal floor of the Commons, to the traditional leader's room which Thatcher and Kinnock had occupied, whilst John Prescott took over John Smith's old office upstairs.[71] The scene on the first few days of the new leadership was described by Alastair Campbell, whose visit to be offered a job by Blair on 27 July 1994 was recorded in his published diaries:

> TB called and asked me to go and see him in the shadow Cabinet room. I arrived at 1.30 and into the kind of turmoil you normally associate with moving house. Boxes and crates of John Smith's papers and possessions on the way out, TB's on the way in, and nobody quite sure where everything should go, and all looking a bit stressed at the scale of the task. Anji Hunter and Murray Elder were in the outer office. . . Tony's own office was in even greater chaos than the outer office so he was working out of the shadow Cabinet Room.[72]

As he noted, Anji Hunter swiftly took up the key position in the outer office immediately adjoining the leader's, whilst other aides worked in the general office in the wood-panelled former study next to the shadow Cabinet room. The geography of the suite briefly became the subject of low-level political intrigue when a pair of Conservative researchers was expelled from

---
70. *Blair*, Anthony Seldon (Free Press, 2005)
71. *The Times*, 29 September 1994 and *Mail on Sunday*, 2 October 1994
72. *The Blair Years: Extracts from the Alastair Campbell Diaries*, Hutchinson (1997)

the Commons by the Speaker, after being caught by security staff snooping around in Blair's outer office one evening.[73]

Blair's office itself was described by one journalist at the time as a 'bare, functional room which says "I do not intend to be here long."'[74] It was also noted that during meetings he was always to be found on the sofa, a habit which famously translated to government. MPs meeting the leader on routine business in his office were also often nonplussed to find Peter Mandelson sitting in on their discussions there.[75]

Shadow Cabinet met on a Wednesday at 5p.m., preceded by a meeting in Blair's office of the inner circle of John Prescott, Gordon Brown and Robin Cook.[76] In the shadow Cabinet room itself, a bronze of Clement Attlee sat on the mantelpiece, along with a stack of books including the New Testament.[77] *The People* newspaper reported that in September 1996 Blair chose the relative calm of the 'deserted shadow Cabinet room . . . where New Labour was born' to prepare his final Party Conference speech before the general election. The newspaper described a romantic vision of the Prime Minister-in-waiting 'alone with his thoughts', 'out of the spotlight' with 'the only sound the scratching of Tony's pen'. And, presumably, the sound of the camera shutter and flash from the photographer sent along to record the occasion.[78]

William Hague: 1997–2001

When William Hague took over the Conservative Party following the leadership election in July 1997, the task he faced was immense. He recalled:

---

73. *Daily Mail*, 14 December 1994
74. John Rentoul, *The Independent*, 13 July 1996
75. John Rentoul, *Tony Blair, Prime Minister* (Time Warner, 2001)
76. Rentoul, *The Independent*, 13 July 1996
77. The *Sunday People*, 26 February 1995; *The Observer*, 22 October 1995
78. *The People*, 29 September 1996

We hadn't been in opposition for nearly twenty years, so most members of the Party didn't have any recollection of being in opposition... There were no people sitting in an office waiting to say 'this is what we're going to say today'. Now that's fine – I knew that was the position. Somebody has to take hold and say 'right – you come and work for me; you come and work for me; get those phones installed, start answering the letters'. [79]

His staff in fact lost no time in taking over the opposition's offices in the Commons – so much so that when some of John Major's outgoing private office staff came in the following day to clear their desks, they found their belongings had already been cleared out by the over-eager new regime.[80]

Hague chose not to move into the traditional leader's office on the principal floor, but instead occupied the larger room on the floor above which John Smith had used. The pressure of space in the opposition's offices remained a key issue, still causing some degree of tension.

For his immediate private office staff, Hague drew substantially on those who had worked on his campaign team, and were close personal allies. Charles Hendry, an MP who had lost his seat in the 1997 election, became Chief of Staff, with Sebastian Coe – another parliamentary casualty of the landslide – as his deputy. This arrangement lasted until the end of the year, when Hendry moved to a post in Conservative Central Office, and Coe became Chief of Staff (re-titled Private Secretary). George Osborne, who had been Hague's speechwriter, became his political secretary.

Six months into his leadership, William Hague took the decision 'to integrate his private office more closely with Conservative Central Office' and in January 1998 moved the primary base of his office from the leader's rooms in the

---
79. William Hague, interviewed by Michael Cockerell for *How to be Leader of the Opposition*, BBC (1999)
80. Interview with former staff member, July 2006

Commons to Central Office in Smith Square. Under the new arrangements, his office operated from Smith Square until 2p.m. on days when the House of Commons was sitting, when it moved over to the Commons for the rest of the day. It seems Hague and his team were consciously seeking to model their operations on the conduct of government, and even commissioned a number of 'red boxes' from the company which makes them for the government. These were covered in dark blue leather instead of red, and embossed with the words 'leader of the opposition' with a parliamentary portcullis crest instead of the Royal Arms. These were used in exactly the same way as in a ministerial private office, with briefings, memos, letters for signature and other material placed inside for the leader to work on in the evenings and at weekends. Just as in Whitehall, the private office began to enforce a rigid discipline of deadlines for submissions to the leader, with a cut-off point in the evenings when 'the box closes'.[81]

Although the new arrangements were designed to increase co-ordination between the leader's office, Central Office and the shadow Cabinet, there were criticisms that Hague's team were too cliquey. Lord Parkinson, Hague's first Party Chairman, is known to have found the leader's office less accessible than he would have liked, and others at CCO regarded them with suspicion, particularly the protective role played by Coe.[82] John Redwood, a member of Hague's shadow Cabinet, was said to share these concerns, according to his former political assistant, Hywell Williams:

> He maintained his doubts about Hague's close and introspective circle of advisers. 'You could feel that they were everywhere' he said afterwards, evoking the scene in the leader's office as he strode in to assume a new courtier's role.[83]

---
81. Private source
82. Nadler (2000)
83. *Guilty Men* (Aurum Press, 1998) p.231

This feeling is hardly unusual in such circumstances, but is likely to have been exacerbated by the physical remoteness of the leader's office being based primarily in Central Office. Whilst the leader's suite in the Commons was largely self-contained, the physical reality of being located there, and the presence of other senior colleagues in the 'shadow Cabinet block' off Speaker's Court, afforded greater opportunity for informal contacts with other MPs and a sense of greater accessibility to the leader. Locating the leader and his key staff in Central Office, an institution which evoked long-standing connotations of untrustworthiness and even contempt amongst Conservative MPs, cannot have helped Hague's team as they tried to foster harmonious relations with the shadow Cabinet and Parliamentary Party. The dangers of a 'bunker mentality' developing were heightened, and grew further under the ill-fated leadership of Hague's successor.

Iain Duncan Smith: 2001–2003

Iain Duncan Smith's accession to the leadership of the opposition was delayed by 24-hours following the appalling events of 11 September 2001, and the decision to postpone the announcement of the result of the leadership election in their aftermath. It is therefore perhaps understandable that when he took over on 13 September his staff were as impatient to get started as were William Hague's four years previously. Nevertheless, the sight of Duncan Smith's key lieutenants appearing and milling around excitedly in the leader's outer office in Smith Square within minutes of the leadership declaration was too much for one of Hague's outgoing staff, who promptly left Central Office in tears, past banks of photographers and news crews, to drown her sorrows with friends in the nearby Marquis of Granby pub.[84]

This was a fittingly inauspicious start to the private

---
84. Personal account

office arrangements under 'IDS', which during his brief tenure became the subject of intense political controversy, media scrutiny, and an investigation by the Parliamentary Commissioner for Standards which hastened the troubled leader's departure. That investigation eventually cleared Duncan Smith of wrongdoing over the employment of his wife, but does provide a wealth of first-hand evidence about the set-up of the private office from the people who worked there, from the leader himself downwards.

Duncan Smith records 'there were no staff in the leader's office when I took over apart from the correspondence unit attached to the leader's Office in CCO and a speechwriter in CCO. All of Mr Hague's staff had left the Commons offices as per usual. I did not second staff to the office and there was no "bedrock of support" awaiting me. I didn't even have any proper furniture in my office.'[85] Although he uses the phrase 'as per usual', the situation in which he found himself was fairly unique – as we have seen, many previous leaders taking over whilst already in opposition inherited at least a skeleton staff from their predecessors, and others who had been in government had personal staff who moved with them to opposition. Elsewhere in his statement, he notes that: 'There were numerous staffing changes as a result of the need to establish the leader's office from scratch. These are political appointments so one does not have the civil service the way one would if one were an incoming prime minister.'[86]

The contrast he draws with the immediate support provided for the Prime Minister was particularly stark, given the grave international situation being faced when he assumed the leadership. The following day he was due to make his first appearance at the despatch box of the recalled House of Commons, to respond to the Prime Minister's statement on the

---

85. Written Statement by Mr Iain Duncan Smith, 9 December 2003: Committee on Standards and Privileges, Fourth Report of Session 2003–04 (HC 476–II, House of Commons, 29 March 2004)
86. Ibid.

9/11 terrorist attacks. As a result, his office was hurriedly set up in the vacated leader's office at Smith Square. His parliamentary office in the Norman Shaw North outbuilding was packed up, and the contents delivered to the shadow Cabinet block, where the crates were stored in rooms on the top floor until the new team decided which offices they would occupy.[87]

Duncan Smith's first appointment was Annabelle Eyre, who had been his constituency secretary since 1997, and who now became Private Secretary to the leader. She also remarked on the fact that the office was set up 'from scratch' with no staff or handover notes left behind from Hague's team, and that 'Iain's office had to be transformed from the office of a frontbench parliamentarian to that of the alternative Prime Minister and that it took some time for the arrangements to settle down'.[88]

Christine Watson assumed Eyre's former role as constituency secretary, whilst Andrew Whitby-Collins, who had assisted with the leadership campaign, became diary secretary. Initially, Stephen O'Brien acted as Chief of Staff, until the appointment of Jenny Ungless after the Party Conference in October 2001. There was initially some confusion about the exact structure of the office, with one staff member, Simon Gordon, explaining 'A number of people raised the issue of job titles. I do not know if they raised it with Mr O'Brien but they certainly raised it with his successor, Jenny Ungless, and I think that people were usually told, "That will be sorted out on a future occasion" or "We are not great ones for job titles" or something.'[89] Mr Gordon's own time in the office was short, ending with his being laid off after just four months in January 2002 when the job he had expected to do failed to materialise.[90]

---

87. Written Statement by Miss Annabelle Eyre, 12 November 2003: Committee on Standards and Privileges, Fourth Report of Session 2003–04 (HC 476–II, House of Commons, 29 March 2004)
88. Ibid.
89. Interview with Mr Simon Gordon, Ibid.
90. Ibid.

Others, such as correspondence secretary Adrian Muldrew, have described the initial months of Duncan Smith's private office as being a period of 'anarchy', where 'things were not being done, people outside the inner core were noticing that an awful lot of business was simply not being addressed despite repeated pleas with the inner office to get them addressed'. He recalls 'There was a sort of barrier which immediately went up between the absolute inner core of the leader's office, which was the leader himself, Miss Eyre and Mr Whitby-Collins and the rest of the staff.'[91] It seems that during the leadership campaign there had been a plan formulated by Duncan Smith's campaign manager David Maclean as to how the office would operate, but this was not followed, causing considerable friction.[92]

Just under a year later, there was a significant reorganisation of the office, with Jenny Ungless resigning as Chief of Staff, and Annabelle Eyre moving from being Private Secretary to become Head of Planning and Tours. Her place as Private Secretary was taken by Christine Watson, but the post of Chief of Staff remained unfilled. Iain Duncan Smith recalls that he did not want to fill the post immediately until he had worked out what he wanted from the role. Eventually, Tim Montgomerie was appointed with the title 'Political Secretary', whilst Vanessa Gearson was appointed as 'Administrative Head of the Leader's Office'.

The acrimony which characterised relations between members of the private office at this time is evidenced by the claims and counter-claims in the statements and interviews they gave to the Parliamentary Commissioner for Standards during IDS's investigation. What is not in dispute is that the operation of the leader's office remained characterised by a lack of proper organisation. The Commissioner reported 'There is ample evidence that the roles of staff in

---
91. Interview with Mr Adrian Muldrew, Ibid.
92. Ibid.

the leader's office were initially confused. . . It is also clear that the functioning of the office was suboptimal and that it continued to be less than satisfactory until, at the earliest, the autumn of 2002.'[93]

He then cited evidence from Stephen Gilbert, who commented on the initial period that: 'I do not think anybody is going to pretend... that it [the leader's office] was in good shape, that it was working well... it was not a smooth running operation... although there were some good talented people there, the roles were very ill-defined and people did not really know what their job was, and this resulted in some particular operational difficulties.'[94] Alistair Burt MP, who was not appointed a parliamentary Private Secretary until October 2002, said of his experience of the office: 'I was genuinely taken-aback at the lack of organisation in the running of his office and in the relationship between his office and Central Office.'[95]

The vote of no confidence in Iain Duncan Smith by his own MPs in October 2003 brought his leadership to an end, along with the sorry saga of his private office arrangements. It may simply be that the intense scrutiny resulting from the investigation highlighted tensions and organisational issues which remained largely hidden under other leaders, but his tenure nevertheless stands out as a stark illustration of the effect office politics can have on wider politics, and remains a warning to his successors of the dangers of getting it wrong.

Michael Howard: 2003–2005

With Michael Howard's unopposed selection as leader, Conservative MPs sought to put the traumas of the recent

---
93. Committee on Standards and Privileges, Fourth Report of Session 2003–04 (HC 476–II, House of Commons, 29 March 2004)
94. Ibid.
95. Ibid.

past behind them. Howard himself made an immediate break with the past by rejecting the opposition's rooms in the Palace of Westminster and moving instead into a new suite on the second floor of the Norman Shaw South parliamentary outbuilding, which had just re-opened after undergoing refurbishment. This at least meant that Iain Duncan Smith's reported reluctance to leave the old leader's office for several months did not cause immediate problems, despite pressure from the whips.[96] Eventually he departed and was replaced by Theresa May, who occupied the room until after the 2010 election, when she moved to the Home Secretary's room, which was of course itself the original leader of the opposition's office.[97]

The new suite in Norman Shaw South was more spacious and airy than the 'cramp and conspiracy' of the Palace of Westminster. Rooms opened off a wide L-shaped corridor in which there was a sofa for guests to sit and wait. Howard's own office was established in a large corner room overlooking the Thames, with a conference table and easy chairs as well as a desk. One set of double doors opened straight from the corridor, whilst another set led to the private office next door. An open-plan office for staff was located next door to Howard's room, whilst smaller offices for key advisers led off the corridor. Overall, the whole arrangement was much more akin to the layout and feel of a ministerial suite in a government department.

As his Chief of Staff, Howard appointed Stephen Sherbourne, an experienced political operator who had been political secretary to Margaret Thatcher before moving into public relations. He was joined by Guy Black, the former Director of the Press Complaints Commission, who became Press Secretary, and a number of other heavyweight appointments followed. The contrast with the chaos of

---
96. *Daily Telegraph*, 17 January 2004
97. Personal knowledge

Duncan Smith's time led some commentators to remark that 'the grown-ups are back in charge'.

Despite failing to win the 2005 election eighteen months later, Howard can look back on his time as leader with satisfaction in at least one respect. Not only had he restored discipline and professionalism to his party's operation, but he had succeeded in establishing a vastly improved office environment from which to take on the government. Whilst shadow Cabinet meetings continued to be held over in the House of Commons, the Norman Shaw South building became the seat of the official opposition.

David Cameron: 2005–2010

On becoming leader, David Cameron moved into Norman Shaw South, but the transition was not without difficulty – the House authorities initially tried to remove the extra phone lines installed under Michael Howard and make Cameron's staff re-apply for them.[98] The often absurd logistical problems which face all new oppositions were clearly alive and well.

For his core team, Cameron brought in many close colleagues and long-standing friends who had helped run his successful leadership campaign, such as Edward Llewellyn as his Chief of Staff, and George Eustice as Press Secretary. Many members of Michael Howard's staff also remained in post, notably Private Secretaries Peter Campbell and Jonathan Hellewell. The team Cameron assembled was remarkably cohesive, and survived until the general election.

Shadow Chancellor George Osborne and his staff were also closely integrated into the leader's office, occupying adjacent offices within the Norman Shaw suite. Head of the Policy Review Oliver Letwin was the only other shadow Cabinet member to have a similarly influential position, with an office across the corridor. Most of the other senior members of the

---
98. Private information

shadow Cabinet were next door in Portcullis House, whilst others including David Davis (and later Dominic Grieve), Alan Duncan and Andrew Mitchell inhabited the old 'shadow Cabinet block' near the old leader's office.

The coalition negotiations following the 2010 election meant that David Cameron's tenure in the opposition's offices was extended by some days. Unusually, the parliamentary estate became part of the story of the transition of power. At least one of the crucial meetings in the formation of the coalition took place in the shadow Cabinet room, and Cameron continued to meet colleagues and advisers in his parliamentary office. When Gordon Brown resigned and the call came from Buckingham Palace, it was from Norman Shaw South that David Cameron set out to see the Queen before heading onto Downing Street.

Conclusions

What does this tale of people and places tell us about opposition? There are several things that seem to be important. Most striking is the constant theme of unsatisfactory resources. There is never enough room or enough staff, it seems. Despite the increased workload, with added pressures from the media and public, a constant factor has been the disparity between the demands of the job and the resources and office space available to fulfil it. From Churchill purchasing the house next door to accommodate his secretaries to Gaitskell moving the office wall, to the wholesale office moves of Thatcher and Howard: all have demonstrated the added logistical pressures which an opposition has to overcome before it can even begin to operate on the political level.

Secondly, there is the constant reinvention of the structures of each new leader's office, often with little continuity or pattern to guide it. Iain Duncan Smith's description of having to create his office 'from scratch' is given by him as a mitigating factor for the problems which beset his staff arrangements later on, and other leaders' experiences also bear out the fact that the lack of a pre-existing structure or blueprint for the job has proved to be an immense challenge. Tony Blair's reported comment about the leap from shadow spokesman to leader being harder than that from leader to prime minister is an intriguing insight from one of only three people alive who are in a position to make the comparison.

The assertion does however seem logical. Whilst an incoming prime minister has both the resources and the experience of the civil service machine to draw on, an incoming leader of the opposition has no such advantage, and must rely on the people they themselves put in place, who may be just as overwhelmed by the hugely increased profile and workload they face. The effective operation of the opposition depends on the leader and their staff creating an office structure to meet the needs of the role, but the fresh start under each new leader means there is no real 'institutional memory' built into the system.

Finally, there is the impact on the personalities involved. The lack of rigid structures and the smallness of the leader's office mean that the impact of personal relationships is amplified in opposition. When there is a personality clash, such as with Marcia Williams or with Duncan Smith's staff, the problems take on much more significance because of the relative lack of institutional structures to constrain them.

Office politics matter in opposition because of their impact on the effective running of the leader's team, and the knock-on effect this has on the performance of the whole frontbench. But they matter also because of the impact they have on setting working practices and personal spheres of influence which then translate into government. Tony Blair's 'sofa' style, the 'gatekeeper' role of Anji Hunter, and his reliance on Alastair Campbell, Jonathan Powell and Peter Mandelson first occurred in the Commons, not at Downing

Street. The most influential figures in No. 10 today are those who worked most closely with David Cameron before he came to power. It is not just policy that is developed in opposition.

4. Leading the Opposition

Neil Kinnock

Neil Kinnock led the Labour Party from 1983–1992, fighting two general elections as leader of the opposition. The following is an edited transcript of an interview he gave for my PhD thesis, amended with his approval to make sense with my questions removed. His thoughts on the experience of leading the opposition, told in his distinctive voice, are fascinating and refreshingly honest, and it is a privilege to bring them to a wider audience.

There are many challenging things about being leader of the opposition, but amongst the many varied duties is that you are obliged on a fairly regular basis to go to Buckingham Palace for banquets in honour of visiting heads of state. It doesn't sound particularly onerous, and admittedly the hospitality is lavish, but I never really enjoyed them.

They are quite bizarre occasions. At the end, when dinner is finished, you suddenly hear in the distance the skirl of pipes, and out of nowhere come the Scots Guards, the Irish Guards, the Gordon Highlanders or some other soldiers with busbies and big boots, with six pipers playing as they march around the table. I used to look at the faces of visiting dignitaries who hadn't been warned, and saw many were absolutely terrified. They didn't know what the hell was happening and, given the political climate in some of their countries, wondered whether there was perhaps a coup in progress.

On one of these occasions – a banquet for the King of

Morroco – Glenys and I were milling around afterwards having a cup of coffee, when one of the stewards came up and told us the King would like to speak to me. We went over to where he was sitting, surrounded by his aides and military personnel. 'I know we're going to have a conversation tomorrow,' he said, 'but I couldn't wait any longer to have your description of what really constitutes the function of Her Majesty's Loyal Opposition.'

I was rather taken aback by such a basic enquiry, but did my best to answer it. The 'loyal' part, I told him, comes from the fact that there is no deviation from the standards of respect and patriotism for the monarch, and it doesn't matter whether you're the government or the opposition, you are at one over that. Secondly, the opposition in the United Kingdom is expected to make itself a credible, instantaneous alternative government if events develop in a way that makes that necessary, either by abandonment by the government or defeat at an election. The British people must be presented with a choice of alternatives which can be different in everything but quality. That then means, of course, that you can attack the government unremittingly, and the government can attack you the opposition unremittingly, and as long as there's no resort to violence, just about anything is acceptable.

He listened with rapt attention as I spoke, and then nodded slowly. 'Yes. Thank you very much for that. But I think it might be some time before we introduce it in Morocco.'

It is reactions like that which demonstrate the importance of loyal opposition to a democratic political system, and how fortunate we are to be able to take it for granted in this country. But strangely enough, I had exactly the same conversation with a group of senior US Democrats in Congress in 1990. They were in desperate straits, having been through Reaganism, then Bush the elder, and were really asking what they were going to do to get back.

After acknowledging the gigantic difference between

Congressional and parliamentary democracy, I suggested the first thing they had to do was form a political party that didn't only exist at election time. Then, to choose amongst them a leadership so that everybody would know that this person speaks at all times on behalf of the Democratic Party. By doing that, I told them, you'll be able to achieve an understanding amongst the American people that there is an alternative for the White House, for the Senate, and for the House of Representatives. They also had to work like an opposition, I suggested, which is actually very difficult because all of them in the House and in the Senate are actually part of the government. One of the leading Senators nodded and said 'Well, I think that would be perfect if we could get it, especially about being a real political party instead of a fanclub, but I think it'll be some time before we get that in the United States of America.' I agreed with him, and we went off for a drink.

Whether in Morocco or the United States, it seems, the British concept of opposition can be something of a curiosity.

Frontbench

I first joined the opposition frontbench under Jim Callaghan, following our defeat at the election in 1979. He had announced to the Parliamentary Party that he would be staying on for a period of time because, as he saw it, the Party needed to catch its breath as we adapted to being out of power. But although he fulfilled the role of leader of the opposition, he made it clear there would be some Tuesdays and Thursdays when he wouldn't do Prime Minster's Questions (which he always considered to be overrated), and didn't intend to be a 'jumping up and down' kind of leader. There were people in the Party who expressed doubts over that, but generally speaking, they were the usual suspects – people who were antagonistic towards him in any case.

Even though my politics were pretty divergent from Jim's in some ways, I always had huge respect and affection for him. He had been around a long time, and I think he was probably quite right to go for a more restrained version of parliamentary leadership, to give everyone time to think about what happens next. That was his demeanour – he was pretty laid back, at least on the surface.

When we got to the Labour Party Conference of that year, 1979, 'Bennery' was at its most fevered pitch. Jim got completely brassed off, and I remember as we were walking into an executive meeting on the Wednesday night, he said to me 'I'm going to resign'. He didn't think the Party could ever begin to sort itself out until there had been some kind of trauma, and he intended to provoke that. I, and others from across the Party, told him that was the last thing we needed, and kept on at him to stay, which of course he then did for another year. But all the time, whilst he always sustained a sense of real responsibility, he wanted the cup to be taken from him.

In those days there were twelve places to be elected in the shadow Cabinet. I stood, and out of nowhere came thirteenth by about two votes. On the strength of that, Jim offered me what in Labour Party terms was a very significant portfolio: education. That irritated some elements on the so-called right of the Party, because I hadn't been elected, but the following year I was very safely elected, so they didn't have that bee in their bonnet after that.

It was then a case of starting to get a policy process going, because the last two policy initiatives under the Labour government had been Jim's famous education speech in Ruskin College Oxford, and Shirley Williams's efforts to advance non-selective secondary education, and that was about it. There wasn't an awful lot in the way of policy. The NEC would have liked to run the whole process themselves, but I couldn't work like that. It had to be my education policies, not through any sense of egotistical proprietorship, but simply because if I wasn't in charge of the policy process, there *was* no policy process. A thousand flowers would have bloomed and, as Chair of the Home Policy Committee of the NEC, Tony Benn would have been in charge of that, like he was just about everything else. But I was lucky that there was at that time an education officer of the Labour Party, an excellent guy called Bert Clough, and Charles Clarke became my part-time researcher, so I at least had two decent policy people to work with. We produced our own 'White Papers' on issues like the treatment of private schools, 16–19 education, and the curriculum. Some of it is pretty orthodox thinking now, but was quite cutting edge then.

I was also fortunate in being one of the first generation to get so-called 'Short Money', named after Ted Short. I gave it all – about £5,000 I think – to Charles Clarke, who put food on his table by a mixture of maths teaching, his allowances as Chairman of Housing in Hackney, and the Short Money from me. It never amounted to much, but it meant Charles could work for me without starving.

Some other portfolios could rely on substantial help with research expenditure from trade unions, whereas education, by definition, was largely non-affiliated union territory. If I had an explicit research request they never turned it down, but no union was writing cheques for maintaining an education researcher. In some areas of policy they did, and of these, transport was the outstanding case. John Prescott as Transport spokesman had money coming out of his ears, which was the subject of some merriment – it was one of my favourite riffs in shadow Cabinet to tell jokes about how much money the unions were giving John, which he always resented, but it caused a little diversion at tense times.

We then came to preparing the 1983 manifesto. The policy process in the Labour Party is provided for in the Constitution, where Clause Five states that, in order to draw up 'the Party programme for the election' as it was called, there had to be a meeting between the National Executive Committee and the Parliamentary Committee of the Labour Party. This 'Clause Five meeting' conventionally took place a day or two after an election was declared.

The 1983 one was peculiar in that no manifesto was written. There was a Party programme that had been endorsed the previous autumn at the Labour Party Conference – a long rambling document outlining policy in great detail – but it was totally unsuited to being a manifesto. The Clause Five meeting was held in a committee room of the House of Commons in conditions of great gloom, because everybody going into that meeting knew we were going to get beaten, and the only question was by how much.

I knew that we would become even less credible in the election if we went round with this huge Old Testament tome that actually said nothing: it had two pages on fox hunting and the word 'computer' did not appear in the whole document. So I wrote a note to Michael Foot saying 'We can't fight on this document – why don't you suggest a few of us take it away and slim it down?'

Michael sent a note back to me saying he daren't open it up at all because, looking around the room, he could see what the majority was like and knew they would add in all kinds of nonsense. So in the shortest Clause Five meeting in history, the proposal was made that we adopt as the Labour manifesto the Party programme agreed by the previous Labour Party Conference. And that was how what Gerald Kaufman called 'the longest suicide note in history' became, every last word of it, the 1983 manifesto.

Was that election unwinnable? The condition of the Labour Party at the time certainly made the job of the Conservatives easier – they could scarcely believe their luck. But there were several other factors: when she was first elected, Mrs Thatcher's majority wasn't very big, there was serious division within the

Conservative Party, and she was not highly regarded by the public as a Prime Minister. People think it was the Falklands that changed that, but it wasn't that simple. After what I used to call the slaughter of the innocents – the eradication of 25 per cent of United Kingdom's manufacturing capacity and the massive rise in unemployment – the recovery had started in late 1981, and there was starting to seep through what I termed the 'feelgood factor' (a familiar term now, but one which I first used at that time).

That feeling had already started, and it went on developing. Then the emotion attendant upon the Falklands seemed to epitomise the virtue of strong, stubborn leadership. We can argue about the rights and wrongs of that conflict, but the most important thing is that the perception was of a triumph, and that's when something called 'Thatcher*ism*' was born. So we had the 'feelgood factor' emerging because of the gradual upturn in the economy; then the morale boost of the Falklands; and on top of that the split in the Labour Party, the formation of the SDP and the fact that it seemed we couldn't see a single mistake without wanting to return to it. Put those things together and you've got an inevitable result, made even stronger, maybe by a factor of 10 or 15 per cent, by circumstances outside of Margaret Thatcher and the Conservative Party.

Being leader

When I became leader in the wake of our defeat in 1983, I was well aware of the huge challenges the Party faced. My main feeling was 'well, I can't complain from here on in – I've just got to bloody well get on with it'. The circumstances were not propitious, and in many respects I was quite despairing about the policy stance of the Party and the reputation that we had built for ourselves. But it had to be done, simple as that.

Don Concannon, a dear friend of mine who had been my

flatmate for two years when I was first in Parliament, gave me some good advice. He was a coalminer from Nottinghamshire, an ex-soldier and a man of immense personal courage who became a great Minster of State for Northern Ireland. He said to me in a spirit of really avuncular advice: 'Two innings match, son – and you'd do bloody well if you do it in two innings. But it's doable.' That actually defined precisely what I was trying to get my hands around in terms of the scale of the challenge.

What I couldn't anticipate at the time was that the first 'innings' would give the other side a lead that I couldn't guess at. That was largely due to the fact that we couldn't change policies – including crucial policies like unilateral nuclear disarmament – fast enough. But the main difficulty confronting us as it turned out between 1983 and 1987 was the twelve, eighteen, maybe even twenty-four months that we lost to the lead up to, occurrence of, and aftermath of the year-long miners' strike. It was the only show in town, and you couldn't make anything else happen in the Labour Party at the time. The only really significant changes I was able to make were to end our opposition to council house sales, and to make it very, very clear that we were no longer in favour of pulling out of the European Union, and were in fact a 'pro-European' party.

They were the only significant policy changes, and they had to be carefully navigated, so they were barely noticed. They didn't do us any harm, but they didn't do us much good either. The Tory lead at the 1987 election should really have been about twenty-one smaller than it was: we gained twenty-one seats, but we should have gained forty-two.

The miners' strike was bad for us in several ways. First, the news reporting meant the public saw the word 'Labour' and immediately thought of coal mines and flying pickets. Secondly, the Labour movement absolutely turned in on itself. People didn't want to talk about anything other than the miners' strike – who was on whose side, what the outcome was going to be, and the civil liberties questions. Lastly and most damagingly, that uproar reminded people of the 'Winter of Discontent'. Here was old film of mouldering piles of rubbish with rats running through it just a few years before, and here was brand new film of miners clashing with police in a medieval battle – and it was all 'Labour'. There was perpetual evocation of all those things over that eighteen month period, and Labour – its policy processes, its membership, its MPs – all trod water.

There was a deeper cultural problem in the Party too. There were some words that were abominated in certain sections of the movement at that time. Words like 'mainstream', 'relevant', 'modern' or 'forward-looking'. If you used those, the ultra-left dismissed you as someone who was suffering from 'electionitis' – an unhealthy preoccupation with getting votes. Most reasonable people would expect a political party to have at least a passing interest in getting votes, but that is not how many on the left viewed things.

A marooned political party is rather like a religious sect – it takes comfort in the idea that one day those poor benighted people out there will see the true light, and understand that we, the Party, are correct. 'We are the people with the insights,' they think, 'we are the people with the wisdom, and therefore we should talk to ourselves, because no one else will understand us, poor things.' Or at least if you are a progressive party you say 'poor things' – if you're a regressive party you say 'curse them' – that's the only difference. In both cases it's nonsense, and irrelevant to the needs and aspirations of the public. But that's where too many in the Labour Party were in the mid-1980s.

Worse still, for extremists like those in Militant and the rest of the ultra-left, their position wasn't even as thoughtful as that – it was pure self indulgence. It wasn't just that they thought that the Labour Party shouldn't chase after votes; it was that they had contempt for adjusting policies in order to gain public recognition and support. They thought it was a real departure from the function of politics, which to them was to provide people with big mouths to preach. Then if they occasionally got executive power in a union or in a bit of the country, these people, who we might call 'political hobbyists' used to indulge their hobby in the way they did in Liverpool, in parts of London and a few other places in the United Kingdom.

Inevitably, what they were doing was seized upon by the press and represented as if it was typical of Labour, when actually it was eccentric by Labour standards, let alone anybody else's. I knew that wasn't the majority feeling in the Labour movement because the people I knew – the decent Labour core – didn't feel like that. The victory had to be gained for being modern and being relevant, and it had to be gained as quickly as possible over a broad front. Otherwise, we were just a debating club, and not a very good one at that.

If people are serious believers that there is a better, more decent, fairer and more just way of running the country, but are not prepared to develop the policy and win a broader consensus supportive of those beliefs, they shouldn't be in the business at all. Too many people got to the point where they luxuriated in not having any of national governmental responsibility, especially when they could get their ego trips at local level. To be a credible and effective opposition, you have to keep your mind on the main objective – that you have to win power to make any change. If you're not serious about trying to win democratic power, and accepting the discipline of ideas and relations that go with that, then you should go and do something else.

That was the challenge I had throughout my time as leader – to make the Labour Party a credible alternative government. There are several ingredients to that including – crucially – real discipline, identification of priorities, and mobilising people behind those objectives. Those cannot simply be political predilections, they have to be genuine public priorities that get authenticity amongst the political ranks because they're what they hear in their own constituencies and their surgeries, not just what they read in newspaper columns. Finally, when the lull following an election defeat is over, for anything up to three years there has to be a repeated sense of an impending election, which of course helps with the policy formation, and with the discipline.

All those things feed into each other, and whilst they don't guarantee that you're only in opposition for one term (as we discovered), they can make it more purposeful and endurable. Above all, they sustain the legitimacy and relevance of a political party, and make sure it never loses reputation in the public eye. By doing that, you fulfil what in the British constitutional sense is the primary function of the main opposition party, which is to be a government-in-waiting. If you don't look like that, if you don't feel like that, you ain't gonna be it.

Second innings: 1987–92

Our defeat in 1987 was not a great surprise, but the margin of loss still left me depressed and angry. The biggest frustration derived from the fact that most of our wounds and woes were self-inflicted. That isn't to say that no damage was inflicted on us by the Conservatives, or by the Liberals, the SDP or the press – of course that happened too. But damage of the disabling kind, of the kind that really daunts and cows a political party, came from inside. That's what made me so bloody angry, and still does. I think that applies to all oppositions, and to governments too. If you look back over a period in which you can't think of a single significant thing that the other side has done to win extra support, and yet you are still experiencing difficulty, it can only be deriving from inside. Self inflicted wounds in politics are the ones that turn septic most quickly, and where gangrene sets in.

So in that second innings as leader I did start to make more serious reforms to the Party. I firstly cut the staff of the Labour Party, partly as a cost exercise, but also to try and improve the quality of performance by moving people out who weren't making much of a contribution, or who shouldn't have been working for the Labour Party at all. It was a struggle even to get the authority to accomplish that. But slowly and arduously I managed to secure a dependable majority on the National Executive Committee. Without that, a Labour leader couldn't make executive decisions about the Party as an organisation, operate effective machinery for enforcing discipline, or adopt a meaningful policy development process. Other parties are slightly different, but the Labour Party then had real authority vested in the NEC, and so I had to spend time getting control of that.

With that achieved, we were able to begin a proper policy review process. That became, in the first instance, an exercise in stopping being some of the things we had become. We had inflicted so much damage on ourselves over such a long time that there was a real inclination to just say 'let's stop being these things', and hope that would provide sufficient reassurance, which if delivered with passion would gives us a fighting chance. That was a necessary part of the change, but not sufficient.

The second mission was to find the replacements for the central elements of the programme that were not just not negatives, but actual positives for us. That was essential, but it got squeezed out by the sheer length of time taken up by the first part of the process. The business of discharging old policy was tough, not least because political parties are a little like religious sects, and a policy can take on the character of religious conviction. It becomes a Shibboleth. Getting rid of that policy then doesn't just require victory in a practical or intellectual argument, but a dislodging of faith, which is a damn sight more difficult. Even in a party that prides itself on its pragmatism, like the Conservative Party, there are things that, as David Cameron could testify, people will cling onto by their fingernails.

Nevertheless, we did get a process under way, with the policy review groups. In addition, from 1989, there was help from an engine I was substantially responsible for establishing to try to improve policy development capacity, the Institute for Public Policy Research (IPPR). That was never intended to be a subsidiary of or a weapon of the Labour Party, but instead to be an accessible high-grade think tank whose analysis could be depended upon, even when it was disagreed with. I and one or two kindred souls in the TUC set about establishing it within weeks of the 1987 election, with the original conception that it should be a 'commissioning' think tank, so it could get the freshest and best analysis. The advantage for the Party would be that the general disposition of the organisation would be pro-Labour, and whilst the people working for it would know that they shouldn't be inhibited because of that, they should work in the certain knowledge that their reports would find their way onto the leader of the Labour Party's desk.

That was one bit of external machinery that I was able to introduce, and of course it went from strength to strength. At the same time the Party's own policy capacity was strengthened, but it was never strengthened enough to make it authoritative in policy identification and development. I think the Tories have traditionally been stronger in that area, notably with the way their Research Department operated after the war, and with the role the right-wing think tanks played. That was the kind of thing I had in mind, and it would have been a real asset if it had pre-existed, but we had to invent it.

Even after we had developed detailed policy, we were sometimes constrained in how much of it we could reveal ahead of the election. In 1992, for example, I was determined if elected to cut interest rates in half, and to manage the consequent – and vitally needed – fall in the Pound with the assistance of other members of the Exchange Rate Mechanism. The only other alternative as I saw it was to get the Deutschmark revalued, and I knew the Germans would not do that. But I knew they would be quite happy to assist us in managing the fall in the Pound, because it was in their interests to do so. Now, saying to people 'we're going to cut interest rates in half, and this is how we're going to do it' may have been superficially attractive, but we would have been crucified in the election, and portrayed as the party of devaluation.

We also at that stage had great ambitions for the National Health Service. When challenged, we could demonstrate that we could afford it by reference to the form of tax increases that we were going to make, which would have affected a miniscule proportion of British taxpayers and families. The better course in policy terms, which Robin Cook and I favoured, was a 'standard rate' tax cut and introduction of an hypothecated National Health Service and Community Care tax. It was attractive because people would see the connection between what they got and what they spent, but it would also have been represented as 'another Labour tax rise', which would have got completely in the way of the substance and appeal of it, so it couldn't realistically be done. That was one of the biggest dilemmas in opposition – there were policies which were necessary and which you knew would make a truly beneficial change and be a real advantage for the economy and society, but you couldn't campaign on them because they would be misrepresented out of all recognition.

At the same time as developing policy for the next election, we also had to fulfil the primary task of holding the government of the day to account. Parliamentary opposition is the name of the game, so most of the focus has to be on Parliament itself. Although performance in the Chamber is not the be-all and end-all, it has an important function in building a reputation. A good performer in the Chamber, even if losing the vote, can make a difference to the course of events. It is a modern irony that the most avid parliamentarians are the ones who spend the most time attacking it – that is the journalists. Even now in the twenty-first century, they are still the people they were in the 1950s and 1960s, who are essentially sports commentators. They exaggerate both good performances and bad, and they will remember those performances longer than virtually any parliamentarian.

Prime Minister's Questions is of course the most visible occasion of the parliamentary week, and is best used by the opposition to help set the news agenda on their terms. How well you are able to do that depended on the issue, and a little bit on luck. I can give three instances of that from my time as leader, the first of which was the National Health Service. Some people used to think I came back to that because it was an easy issue for Labour and a tough issue for Margaret Thatcher, whilst others knew that I decided upon a fairly explicit strategy of coming back to it again and again. Firstly, because it was a legitimate issue to raise, but secondly, because eventually things would be said that could be contradicted immediately by real experience, preferably with a bit of film. I also had confidence that I had a spokesman in Robin Cook who would never drop the ball, no matter who threw it, and no matter how fast.

The second issue, which eventually we got up and going, was the Poll Tax. In retrospect, people think it was a piece of cake – it was such a categorical error it should have been a push-over – but it wasn't like that. It wasn't until people really started to see it in operation – and not only what it meant in terms of individual liability for tax, but the gigantic size of the bills – that we got it to take off politically. So I used repetition at PMQs and used individual cases when we could. Sometimes it was directly on the Poll Tax, but quite often it was on housing benefit and how people couldn't get help to meet their liabilities, which dramatised it, and I did it remorselessly. I had to make absolutely certain that any case I took up was absolutely bona fide, and that if by some accident it was discovered who I was talking about, the case would stand up. We had be really careful about that, because when you try to personalise a broad political argument, which you have to do more in opposition than in government, you have to make sure it's absolutely sound.

The final area where in the end repetition made a difference, was Nigel Lawson. I just kept on at PMQs, because of the absolutely huge dispute inside the government between Lawson and Thatcher's economic adviser Alan Walters. I just kept on asking about Lawson and, Maggie being Maggie, wouldn't give any hint of a disagreement. She became more and more resounding in her endorsement of policy, but not of the Chancellor. You only had to say 'Alan Walters' to her, and she would immediately spring to his personal defence.

Eventually – I think it was the ninth time of asking – she again failed to endorse Lawson, despite saying a few days earlier that he was 'unassailable'. Lawson signed the previously drafted letter of resignation in the Treasury and took it across to Downing Street, and that was that. I was absolutely delighted, and don't mind admitting we had a few drinks to celebrate that night. None of the basic elements there were of my making, but by drawing attention to it, and by keeping on and on, we were able to exploit the situation.

But of course it's not all set-piece performances in the Chamber that matter. Much of the important work in opposition is behind the scenes: the hard slog in committees, and the fastidiousness of the specialist MP who becomes recognised as an authority in the land, simply by their hard work and insight.

Those things are assisted by an excellent, accessible Library service and by research assistance, but basically it is political inspiration and hard work that gets the job done – nobody else can do it for you. Had there been a few more research assistants and easier access to technology, our performance could have been better, but in the end the ones who were really good were those who mixed talent with hard work. It wouldn't have mattered how many research assistants Denis Healey, Gerald Kaufman, or Bryan Gould had – they were class acts in any case. Better facilities can make the task of being effective easier for an opposition politician, but they don't make the difference between a nonentity and a genius.

Despite the fact that the job of opposition is to oppose, and we took no prisoners in the Chamber or on the airwaves, there were of course more civilised contacts between us and the government. Before the 1992 election there was a formal process of contacts with the civil service to be gone through to ensure they knew our plans and were ready should we have won, and Charles Clarke ran the operation with the Cabinet Secretary. It hadn't happened in 1987, because Mrs Thatcher called the election earlier than the deadline, but in 1992 they were very accommodating and helpful. You would expect that because they're all professionals but, in addition, John Major was in many ways much more grown up about contacts with us than Thatcher. He was under pressure, but he didn't seem to think that if he gave you a confidence about intelligence he was selling his birthright. There were more of these briefings on so-called 'Privy Council terms' when he was Prime Minister, partly because of the Gulf War, and they were always very civilised and – of course – totally secure.

When obliged to, Thatcher had talked to me about Northern Ireland, but it only happened a few times a year, and only when there was either some kind of significant initiative like the Anglo–Irish Agreement, or a particularly fraught security situation. I think she used to embarrass the civil servants at times, because she was always quite 'gung-ho' about the condition of Northern Ireland, when reality – not just tactical common sense, but reality – counselled otherwise. Her briefings on Northern Ireland were never much use – it was much better for me to talk to the Secretary of State or for my shadow spokesman to talk to the civil servants, the police or the army, because they were always very forthcoming, especially if we talked to them in Northern Ireland.

The lessons

The British system of opposition remains remarkably rare. There are near models of it in Australia, both at state and national level, and in Canada and New Zealand. But what has struck me when looking at other systems is that there is no exact replica even amongst the countries that come close to it.

Leading the opposition is certainly a challenging experience, and in my case, one that ended in disappointment. Soon after the 1992 defeat I said I considered myself a personal and political failure. Others endearingly disagreed. But however often I revisit it I still regard myself to be a personal and political failure, because if you lose two elections you'd be a bloody idiot or appallingly arrogant not to think that. I also said I had wasted eight years of my life, but I suppose I would rationalise that now by saying 'someone had to do it'. I'd hoped to waste only four years of my life, but by the time we got to the 1987 election I knew we couldn't win in any case, and the real test was fighting hard enough to convince your own troops that you were in with a real shout. That sadly meant that people were even more distraught in the circumstance of defeat than they would have been otherwise.

In between elections you can, by dint of persistent organisation and force of argument, get the government to shift its position in a positive direction that shows your opposition is working. If you get a couple of those under your belt, it does wonders for your own troops and it really starts the shoulders sagging on the other side. They don't come along very often, and you need more than diligence and imagination and courage to do it: you need some luck as well, or events conspire against you.

But ultimately, the only test of a good opposition is to stop being in opposition. We came much closer in 1992, but any sportsperson who's failed to win a world championship by a few points understands what I felt then more than anybody. I coined a phrase once about the difference between Tony Blair and myself – I made the Party electable; he got the Party elected. And there's a hell of a difference.

5. Painting Their Way Out of the Corner: The Conservatives in Opposition

Tim Bale

Tim Bale is Professor of Politics at Sussex University and the convenor of the Political Studies Association's specialist group on Conservatives and Conservatism. He is the author of The Conservative Party: From Thatcher to Cameron *(Polity Press, 2010).*

> The Conservative Party in opposition resembles some unhappy creature of the deep that has been suddenly and tragically removed from its natural environment and is thrashing around desperately in its bewildered anguish.
>
> Robert Rhodes James, *Ambitions and Realities*, 1972

Given it likes to think of itself as Britain's 'natural party of government', the Conservative Party may indeed find opposition psychologically tougher than its rivals. But if that is the case, it has, at least until recently, made a pretty good fist of it. It took the Party, when led by Winston Churchill, only six years to overhaul the massive majority won by Labour in 1945. Likewise, it was only out of office for six years between 1964 and 1970. True, Ted Heath, who took over from Alec Douglas-Home in the middle of 1965, proved unable to stop Labour's Harold Wilson turning the bare majority he won the year before into one of nearly a hundred in 1966. But that only makes Heath's victory four years later – and the working majority of around thirty it gave him – all the more impressive. Unlike Heath, whose subsequent premiership she regarded as a disaster, or indeed Churchill, who was one of her heroes, Margaret Thatcher managed to win the first (and in her case the only) election she ever fought as leader of the opposition.

It is not entirely surprising, then, that many Conservatives were confident, even after they were so badly beaten by Tony Blair in 1997, that they would be able to turn things around fairly quickly. Labour governments, they reasoned, even if they were successful, soon fell victim to exhaustion and internal division; either that, or they were miserable failures that voters couldn't wait to get rid of. But while this may have been true, it was, they discovered as they went on to lose two more elections, only half right. The Conservative Party in 1951, 1970, and 1979, hadn't returned to office merely by default but also by dint of its own efforts. Moreover, it had done so by following a fairly simple strategy, albeit one capable of being executed in slightly different ways. David Cameron may not have delivered his party an outright majority in 2010 but the fact that he came pretty close owed much to his rejecting the ideological complacency and fatalism of his three immediate predecessors, William Hague, Iain Duncan Smith and Michael Howard, and returning instead to a tried and trusted recipe.

That recipe is far from a closely guarded secret. The basic minimum that British parties thrown out of office have to do in order to recover power is clear. As well as pointing out the error of the current government's ways, the opposition has, first and foremost, to convince the public that it's a safe, centrist, alternative – equipped with a plan, maybe, but a pragmatic one, put together by people who look as if they know where they want to go and where the money's going to come from. A leader who possesses charisma, confidence and just the right amount of conviction is a bonus but projecting decisiveness and competence matters every bit as much. So, too, does the ability to convey the sense that the Party has moved on from when it was last in government. Not only that, the opposition has to show that everyone in its ranks is on board: even though they're not getting all they want from the leadership, MPs and the wider membership have to be motivated – and sufficiently well organised and financed – to get the vote out.

All this of course is easier said than done. Exactly how an individual leader chooses to achieve these goals – if he or she achieves them at all – varies. But the variations are far from infinite. In fact, from an examination of the Tories' four periods in opposition between 1945 and 2010 they can be boiled down to just two options. One is the impressionistic approach outlined by Rab Butler, who, along with Party Chairman Lord Woolton, is generally regarded as having played a crucial role in the Conservatives' recovery after 1945. This is the most popular approach, followed not only by Winston Churchill but also by Margaret Thatcher and, indeed, David Cameron. The other approach – only really followed by one successful Tory opposition leader, Ted Heath – we can label 'pointillism'. In contrast to his impressionist counterparts, the leader who follows this approach relies not on broad brushstrokes but on getting things right in each and every facet of organisation and policy, on the assumption that, taken together, they will constitute a bigger picture which will in the end become clear – and make sense – to voters. Both approaches seem capable of propelling the Party into government, but the less popular of the two would appear to create more problems once power is achieved.

1945–51

Winston Churchill was notoriously reluctant to involve himself in, let alone commit to, detailed policy when in opposition between 1945 and 1951. He also refused to run a shadow Cabinet in the way that we would understand the term today. Instead, members of his 'Consultative Committee' were expected to be able to range across different policies rather than confine themselves to a particular portfolio and, should he decide at the last minute not to lead the charge on a particular Bill, be able at the drop of a hat to step into the breach. Facing a Labour government with a huge majority that was bound to enjoy something of a honeymoon, and desperate both to shore up his income and cement his reputation as a world statesman, Churchill essentially contracted out responsibility for his party's recovery to men he felt he could trust and were clearly well-suited and keen to do the work.

Anthony Eden (Churchill's eventual but not very successful successor) operated as de facto leader in the Commons, while Fred Woolton (building, it's worth mentioning, on the work of his unsung predecessor Ralph Assheton) set about retooling and financially fuelling a machine that had inevitably fallen into disrepair during the war years. Both men were popular with ordinary Party members who were unable to see at close quarters the flaws and foibles that so irritated some of their colleagues. Responsibility for putting together a policy platform that might persuade people that the Tories could live with the post-war welfare state while keeping alive the dream of a less regulated and less heavily-taxed economy was handed to Rab Butler, whose chairmanship of both the Conservative Research Department (CRD) and the Party's Advisory Committee on Policy (ACP) put him in a particularly powerful position, notwithstanding the fact that Churchill retained the final say.

Churchill, it should be said, began to take more interest in what was being done in his name once the Labour government ran into trouble and an election loomed larger. By the time it took place in 1950, the Party's organisational recovery – which, given the return of peace and middle-class resentment over the narrowing of the gap between them and ordinary working people, would almost certainly have occurred with or without Woolton – was complete. Membership tripled after

1945 to over two million. There was also plenty of money, and here Woolton does deserve credit for motivating (and then all but obliging) the constituency associations to stump up extra cash. His fighting fund appeal launched in the autumn of 1947 raised the equivalent in today's prices of £30 million in just one year, while the 'quota' system he helped introduce a little later on helped ensure that the Party was able to make early forays into survey research on floating voters and to spend massively on advertising. Moreover, it was able – just – to maintain its edge over a Labour Party now flush with cash from union backers whose political funds had been swelled by legislation requiring their members to contract out of instead of contracting into the political levy. One can also argue that the Tories' income was better spent, not least when it came to their highly co-ordinated response to the introduction of postal voting – an operation which almost certainly denied Labour what would otherwise have been a comfortable majority in 1950. In the absence of the latter, Attlee was forced to face the country again within eighteen months, ensuring that it was a Conservative rather than a Labour government that was able to profit politically from the post-war boom.

By 1950 and 1951 (when they finally overhauled Labour) the Tories had also restored their other traditional advantage over their rivals, namely the ability to field full-time and mainly fully-trained agents in virtually every single seat in the country. The candidates who fought those seats were not, it should be noted, so very different in terms of background (or gender!) from those who had fought them in 1945. The famous Maxwell Fyfe report that finally stopped associations selling seats to the highest bidder did not usher in a swathe of meritocratic, new men. However, the hype that surrounded the changes (whose biggest impact, in fact, was to force associations to find new ways of raising funds) may have contributed – like its post-war membership drive – to the idea that the Conservatives could still be a party representing all classes and none.

For all the talk of Butler's 'New Conservatism' (not least by Butler himself), the Conservative Party fought the 1950 and 1951 elections on a similar platform to that in 1945. This is partly because the Party's first post-war manifesto included more references to the kinds of policies pursued in the post-war era than is often assumed. But it is also because its manifestos in 1950 and 1951 contained rather more free-enterprise, tax-cutting, and anti-collectivist rhetoric than supposedly patrician Tories like Churchill, Eden and Macmillan were credited with by successors (not least Heath and Thatcher) who were bent on portraying themselves as a break with the past. Furthermore, simply comparing the manifestos causes us to miss many of the most important developments in Tory policy during the five years that followed the end of the war. This was when the Conservative Party came to terms – not altogether enthusiastically but certainly realistically – with the constraints imposed upon it by post-war public opinion and a Labour government determined to implement economic and social policies which could not be easily reversed.

A crude comparison of manifestos also ignores the fact that, for a time at least, the Party – most famously in the *Industrial Charter* of 1947 – moved further onto 'socialist' territory than some Tories were happy with before backing up a little (in, for example, *The Right Road* in 1949) thus arriving at a position that most of them could live with but which could also be sold to an electorate that was still very suspicious of their motives. We also have to recognise that while academics may continue to pore over such documents, the vast majority of voters at the time had only the vaguest inkling of them, even assuming they were in the small minority which, according to contemporary opinion research, had heard of them at all. Far more important in conveying the sense that the Conservatives were not about to turn the clock back to the 'hungry thirties' were candidates' election addresses and election broadcasts which not only attacked Labour's incompetence and extravagance but promised the Party would, at the same time as 'setting the people free' from rationing and doing something about the chronic shortage of housing, maintain full employment and continue to fund the NHS.

1964–70

Whatever else they did during the thirteen years they spent in power after 1951, the Conservatives made sure that they gave the lie to Labour's assertions during that year's general election that a Tory government would dismantle the welfare state and oversee a return to mass unemployment. So, while they were of course disappointed that they were narrowly defeated in 1964, they could be reasonably confident of a return to office sometime soon – if not after the next election then almost certainly the one after that. True, they had, like most governments in power for more than a decade, begun to look tired and even old-fashioned – an impression strengthened by the surprise decision to replace the ersatz aristocrat Harold Macmillan with the genuine article, Alec Douglas-Home, in 1963. True also that their economic strategy and their foreign policy had both ended in tears, one in a dash for growth and flirtation with corporatism that never quite came off and the other in a humiliating rejection by French President de Gaulle of Britain's application to join the EEC. But all this left the Tories temporarily discredited rather than fundamentally distrusted. The main aim, therefore, was to wait for 'the Socialists' (they were never referred to as 'Labour' by Conservatives in those days) to mess up while in the meantime coming up with a platform capable of competing with Harold Wilson's claim that the country could plan its way to a dynamic economy, capable of producing sufficient wealth to allow it to improve health, education and social security.

What many younger Tory MPs quickly came to regard as the main obstacle to achieving this aim – Alec Douglas-Home himself – was fairly quickly removed, although such was the respect for his diplomatic talents that (very unusually for a former leader) he stayed on the team as shadow Foreign Secretary. In his place was chosen – and chosen for the very first time by election rather than the customary process of consultation – someone who would hopefully cope with wily Harold Wilson in the Commons (because he too was a grammar-school-boy-made-good), as well as perform rather better than the hapless Alec Douglas-Home on TV. These hopes were sadly misplaced. Edward Heath rarely got the better of his opponent on the floor of the House and was, with one or two exceptions, as embarrassingly ill-at-ease with the television audience as he was with all but his closest friends and colleagues. What Heath did have, however, was drive and a stubborn determination that he could come up with answers to the country's problems which voters would come to realise were more convincing than the 'government by gimmick' on offer from his Labour opponent.

Heath was no neo-liberal ideologue; it was certainly not part of his plan to allow unemployment to rise to pre-war levels and he believed that government had at least a facilitating role to play. But he was convinced that the British economy must be made more dynamic and competitive, not least to allow it to flourish when, eventually, the UK entered the EEC. This could only happen, he was sure, by properly regulating industrial relations, by offering incentivising tax cuts to the so-called 'pacemakers' without whom no investment and wealth generation could occur. It was also vital to move towards a more 'selective' (as opposed to universal) welfare state that would target only those who really needed help, thereby lowering public expenditure or at least diverting it into areas which would ultimately improve the economy, such as healthcare and (higher) education.

Crucially, however, Heath was not content merely to provide a direction of travel. Given he believed that the country's problems (chronic inflation and inefficiency, low productivity and growth) were not solely the responsibility of militant workers but also dilettante managers, the Conservative Party must point the way by producing detailed, state-of-the-art policies that would allow it, once in office, to swing straight into action. Already put in charge of the policy process under Home, and keen to have something to show voters in an election that, he figured, would come sooner rather than later, Heath tasked a plethora of advisory groups (made up of party representatives and outside experts) with coming up with implementable ideas across the whole range of government activity. By the time Wilson – then at the height of his popularity and fearing (quite rightly) that the economy was about to take a turn for the worse – called the election in the spring of 1966, neither Heath nor his colleagues (also quite rightly) believed they could win it. But the Tory leader was determined to use the occasion not simply to prevent Labour from winning a three figure majority (which he did, just) but to advertise the more detailed and more radical approach that, he felt sure, would win him an election in four or five years' time.

The upside of such an approach – an unusual one in that the Conservatives in opposition normally don't allow a leader (especially one struggling to connect personally with voters) sufficient leeway or time to execute a two-term strategy – is that, by the end of the second term, voters at least recognise the alternative on offer from the opposition. The downside of the approach, apart from the obvious possibility that they might not like what they see, is that, having set out its wares so soon and in so much detail, and having presented them as the only honest way forward, the opposition is likely to find it very difficult (both psychologically and politically) to make adjustments, let alone come up with eye-catching new initiatives, between one election and the other. As Churchill (and Butler too) realised, too many detailed commitments in each and every area, even if, looked at from afar, they came together to produce a coherent, pointillist whole, were likely to severely reduce one's room for manoeuvre.

To be fair, the Conservative opposition was by no means completely constipated between 1966 and 1970. Heath's proposals for trade union, tax and local government reform may have been set in something like stone, but there were issues on which he was able to move – and move in the direction of public opinion. The most obvious of these was immigration. The politics of race threw up problems for both big parties in the 1960s. Labour knew full well that it was suspected of being soft on 'coloured' immigration by the majority of voters who wanted it controlled and if possible stopped altogether. The Conservatives, on the other hand, were vulnerable to a feeling among liberal-minded, mainly middle-class people, many of whom would normally vote Tory, that they cared less than they should about outlawing prejudice and discrimination at home and standing up for the democratic and economic rights of indigenous majorities abroad, most obviously those ruled by white minorities in South Africa and Rhodesia (now Zimbabwe). In government, Wilson attempted to square the circle – and if possible embarrass his opponents – by tightening the law on who could come into the country while simultaneously passing 'race relations' legislation designed to clamp down on discrimination in Britain and taking a tough stance (although not tough enough for some of his supporters) on southern Africa. Heath, knowing many of his MPs (and indeed their voters) held less than enlightened views on such matters, but knowing also that many of his closest colleagues (notably Edward Boyle and his shadow Chancellor Iain Macleod) were convinced liberals, for the most part held his fire – an attitude that in the spring of 1968 persuaded the ambitious shadow Cabinet maverick Enoch Powell to make his so-called 'Rivers of Blood' speech predicting some kind of catastrophe unless Britain could be prevented from becoming a multiracial society. Heath is remembered for his immediate sacking of Powell, with whom he had already fallen out over foreign, defence and economic policy. Fewer people, however, recall that in the light of public (and Party) support for Powell's views, Heath slowly but surely tightened Tory policy on immigration until, by 1970, it stood not so very far away from what his populist rival had called for and, along with the Party's focus on combating rising prices, the unions and welfare waste (and wasters), was almost certainly one of the advantages it enjoyed over Labour at the election that year.

As so often, any advantage the Tories enjoyed on policy was reinforced by their edge over its main opponent when it came to organisation. Like most Conservative leaders, Heath encouraged development in this area but for the most part contracted it out to able lieutenants. Heath had inherited Edward du Cann as Party Chairman from Home, and had never really got on with him. Nonetheless he managed to make a start on streamlining spending and boosting revenue, as well as trying to refresh the candidates' list and improving the pay, conditions and training of agents (who were once again employed in far more constituencies than Labour could manage). This was then taken further by Tony Barber, Heath's own pick for the job. It was Peter Carrington, however, who fronted an appeal for funds in 1967–68 which raised around £30 million at today's prices, about a third of which came from ordinary members, with most of the rest coming from business, which wasn't (as had been feared) put off contributing by disclosure legislation passed by the Labour government. Just as crucial was Michael Fraser, whose joint appointment as deputy Party Chairman and Secretary to the shadow Cabinet, plus his continued oversight of the CRD, made for much closer co-ordination between the professional, parliamentary and voluntary parties. Under Fraser, Central

Office not only upped its spend on opinion research but went much further than ever before in integrating it into its efforts to identify and resource so-called 'critical constituencies' and to structure ever more professional marketing, media and advertising campaigns. It was these that provided Heath with both the confidence and the means by which to plug away on particular issues and target crucial sections of the electorate, notably women and skilled working men. And it was that plugging away which played a big part in ensuring (to everyone's surprise but Heath's and that of his senior team at Central Office) that at the general election of 1970 the Party overcame Labour's substantial parliamentary majority and its apparently unbeatable opinion poll lead.

1974–79

Although Heath had given Margaret Thatcher her first big break by inviting her into the shadow Cabinet in the late 1960s, she didn't think much of him as leader of the opposition and thought even less of him as Prime Minister. His abandonment after 1972 of the market-orientated, smaller state policies she favoured, as well as his humiliation at the hands of the unions, convinced her and others on the right of the need for a firmer presence and for policy that was more resilient for being rooted in a philosophy more fundamental than mere managerialism. His conduct during the two elections of 1974, when he openly flirted with the idea of an all-party government of national unity, only served to confirm those views, and when Thatcher beat him in the leadership contest to which he reluctantly submitted in February 1975, it practically guaranteed that she would attempt to cut quite a contrast with her predecessor.

Yet her claim in 1978 that she had 'changed everything' about her party has to be taken with more than a pinch of salt. In organisational terms there were new faces (or in most cases old faces given a new lease of life) but few changes in practice. In policy terms, the Party did little more (at least in public) than recommit itself to the radical agenda that many Conservatives assumed they had signed up to in 1970 before Heath's u-turns in government went on to make a mockery of their assumptions. What was different, however, was a conscious rejection of Heath's focus on detail and a return to the impressionistic approach preferred by the architects of the Party's recovery in the immediate post-war period.

Although Thatcher was in many ways constrained by the presence – even the predominance – in her shadow Cabinet of men who had served loyally under Heath, she could be sure of gaining their willing consent on one thing. All were agreed that the Party had to avoid going into government, as it had done in 1970, with a set of policies so intricately-woven that it prevented it reacting to new circumstances without giving the appearance of abandoning everything it had campaigned on at the election that had brought it to power. This did not mean, of course, that policy should not be discussed or that no plans should be made. But it did mean that too many concrete public commitments should be avoided.

In fact, Thatcher, like Heath, encouraged the setting up of numerous policy groups, overseen by her ally Keith Joseph. However, unlike him, she ensured that their reports focused as much on establishing principles as working out exactly how they would be put into practice. Just as importantly, their reports were not to be seen as authoritative (especially by the media) and did not feed in any systematic way into the policy-making process further up the chain of command. Moreover, Thatcher herself, both in private and in public, put much greater emphasis on communicating – as a 'conviction politician' – what she saw as the Party's core beliefs: reducing the role of the state, lowering taxation, restoring law and order and Britain's reputation in the world, and (especially after the strike-ridden 'Winter of Discontent' of 1978/79) the need to tame the trade union movement. Instead of an accretion of individual policies building up a picture of the Party's intentions – Heath's pointillist approach – the Party's intentions were made clear but individual policies were more a matter of interpretation. Either that or her colleagues were bounced into formulating policies that were consistent with her supposedly spontaneous (but often highly strategic) public remarks, the most obvious example being the move – made after she expressed her sympathy with those who were 'afraid that this country might be rather swamped by people with a different culture' – to toughen the Party's policy on immigration even further than her deputy (and shadow Home Secretary) Willie Whitelaw was originally planning.

Notwithstanding her preference for impressionism over pointillism, Thatcher was careful to ensure that the things she considered crucial – economic, fiscal and monetary policy – were in the hands of those members of the shadow Cabinet with whom, ideologically, she had most in common, not least Geoffrey Howe and Keith Joseph. This ensured, for instance, that the Party went into the 1979 election with a clear commitment to reducing direct taxation and shifting the burden toward indirect taxes, as well as a conviction that inflation was best tackled by controlling the money supply. On the other hand, she insisted that a publication outlining their thinking, *The Right Approach to the Economy* (1977), was published as a pamphlet which supposedly reflected only the views of the authors rather than the Party as a whole. And she was a sufficiently canny politician not to follow Heath's example in 1970 and rule out any kind of concerted incomes policy. This was in part because she might need one and in part because many of her colleagues (Geoffrey Howe as well as the more centrist Jim Prior) were, like many voters, convinced they would. Even a move to tighten trade union law waited on the Winter of Discontent, after which it became clear that public opinion had shifted on the issue. Thatcher was also pragmatic enough to promise to honour the findings of the Clegg Commission on public sector pay, well aware that this would mean a rise in spending in at least the first year of a putative Tory government. In their *Stepping Stones* strategy, John Hoskyns and Norman Strauss, two of her favourite outriders, had stressed that the nation needed to be turned on to 'turn-around' policies and 'good housekeeping' while the Party was still in opposition, but Thatcher was well aware that any attempt at a really big shift in public opinion would have to wait until she got into government.

The election campaign that took Thatcher to No. 10 was not so very different from the one that Heath had fought less than ten years previously. Again, the Party used its superior resources – this time boosted by the efforts of her dynamic young Treasurer, Alistair McAlpine – to employ the best advertising money could buy. Admittedly, in choosing Saatchi and Saatchi, the Tories went with a much less traditional agency. But their targets (again selected as the result of extensive, and expensive, opinion research) were very similar, although on this occasion first-time voters were as much a focus as women and skilled working men. That said, when it came to changing and then projecting her own image, Thatcher had for some time proved herself far more accommodating than her predecessor to the counsel of professional advisers. This was not perhaps surprising since she was well aware that, like Heath's, her personal ratings were below those of her Party and the incumbent Prime Minister, besides she herself had handpicked Gordon Reece, the Party's Director of Publicity. Other key figures on the organisational side were very much her men too, not least Party Chairman Peter Thorneycroft, whose authority (boosted by his reputation as a 'proto-monetarist' based on his resignation from Macmillan's government over its supposedly lax attitude to public spending), helped her rapidly wrest control of Central Office from the 'Heathmen'. His support, and the backing of Willie Whitelaw, also helped win over the Party in the country, which began to warm to the fact that, at last, they were being led by a Tory leader happy to express, rather than trying desperately to suppress, their values and instincts. And where her writ could not be said to run completely, for example in the CRD, which was still run by the centrist Chris Patten, Thatcher sought alternative sources of advice from the Centre for Policy Studies set up by Keith Joseph, as well as from the neo-liberal think tanks and journalists whose support she saw as essential in winning 'the battle of ideas' against the supposed consensus that had led to national decline. In her mind – and this was the populist message she worked hard to convey – her task was to defend and free the people from the political elite (Tory as well as Labour) who had allegedly foisted that consensus upon them. Along with the collapse of the minority Labour government's claim to be able to handle the unions and the economy, and the Liberals pulling the plug that provided it with precious extra votes in Parliament, it was a stance which proved sufficient to win her a majority of over forty seats.

1997–2010

There is no doubt that the seeds of the landslide defeat the Conservative Party suffered at the hands of Tony Blair's New Labour were sown several years beforehand. By the same token, the Party was to a very great extent the author of its own misfortunes in the years that followed. Part of the Tories' problem under both Margaret Thatcher and John Major was that they began to believe their own propaganda. Rather than realising that their electoral victories in 1983, 1987 and 1992 were contingent affairs – achieved through a combination of astute timing and a Labour opposition widely perceived as both incompetent and out of touch – the Conservatives bought into the myth that they had indeed won the proverbial battle of ideas and thereby converted a basically centrist (if relatively authoritarian) country to shrunken-state neo-liberalism. As a result, instead of offering a change of direction, the Party believed it could, under John Major, get away with offering a change of tone. In fact, by the early 1990s, the public had got pretty much all they wanted from the Conservatives and were looking for a government that was going to invest more in health and education, not one intent on closing coal mines, privatising the railways and the post office, and clamping down yet again on spending. Yet rather than making for the politically more profitable centre, the Conservatives – admittedly constrained by the economy and their own internal rows over Europe – headed for the right-wing hills.

The scale of the defeat the Conservatives suffered in 1997 should have given them pause for thought. That it did not was in no small part due to the fact that Major's resignation precipitated an immediate leadership election. That contest not only landed them with a Thatcherite leader, William Hague, whom the public simply could not take seriously; it also prevented the kind of post-mortem that just might have persuaded them that their problem was their product not just the salesman. As a result, at least a year or two was wasted while the Party, which complacently assumed it had to do little more than say a few superficial *mea culpae* for the sleaze, internal disunity and economic dislocation of the Major years, woke up to the fact that Blair and Brown were delivering the combination of social justice and economic dynamism likely to lead to re-election. Even then, this belated realisation that things would have to change more fundamentally if the Tories were to avoid another rout, was far from widespread. And by that time Hague was as worried about holding on to his job as he was about winning the general election. The problem was that remaining leader involved pandering to the right-wing populist instincts he shared with his party – including its media cheerleaders – whereas convincing voters involved dragging it kicking and screaming into a less obsessive (and more centrist) stance.

With the election of Iain Duncan Smith following another disastrous defeat in 2001 things simply went from bad to worse. And while his replacement by Michael Howard meant that at least the Party's salesman was taken seriously again, its product would prove even harder to change. The only upsides were accidental and longer-term. By doing so badly IDS, like Labour's Michael Foot, probably helped shake the Party out of its complacency, while his embryonic attempts to get it to take social justice seriously sowed some valuable seeds for the future. And by not following Hague and Major and stepping down straight after his election defeat in 2005, Michael Howard handed the Party a breathing space during which David Cameron and his close associates had time not only to win the leadership in December of that year but also to think hard about what they wanted to do with it once it was theirs.

The improvement in Tory fortunes under David Cameron doubtless had a lot to do with the eventual implosion of New Labour under Gordon Brown, a man who, while clearly suited to his job as Chancellor of the Exchequer, should never have been allowed by his colleagues to become Prime Minister. And of course that improvement in fortune was not sufficient to win the Party an overall majority at the general election of 2010. But we should not allow this to obscure the scale of the current Tory leader's achievement. Only four years after taking on the leadership of a despised and derided party, and operating in a system no longer dominated by just two obvious choices as it was in their day, he recaptured more seats than Churchill managed after 1945 and came close to matching the swing that saw Margaret Thatcher safely into Downing Street in 1979. That he did so was down to his following their impressionistic approach to opposition. But it was also because, like them, he listened carefully and scientifically to voters and understood that he had to meet them at least half way.

Without trashing the Party's supposedly glorious past, Cameron effectively distanced himself from it. And, while avoiding out-and-out clashes with the Thatcherite hotheads in his party, and by refusing simply to do the bidding of some of their cheerleaders in the media, he managed to convey the impression that the Conservatives were at last 'fit for purpose' for the twenty-first century.

Cameron's strategy depended on conveying (indeed, on him personally incarnating) change, modernisation, and, most vitally of all, overseeing a move onto the fabled 'centre ground' with a consistency and a coherence, with a will and a wider message discipline, that none of his three predecessors since 1997 had come even close to matching. His election as leader was immediately followed by a series of counter-intuitive initiatives and announcements (on the environment, on big business, and on the NHS), by the dumping of particularly toxic policies and the delaying of all the rest via the setting up of policy groups, and by action on candidate selection (via the so-called 'A-List') to make the Party look at least a little more like the country whose votes it was seeking. There was also no point, Cameron reasoned, in the Party banging its head against a brick wall by trying – in opposition anyway – to convince the electorate (as his predecessors had tried to do) that its much cherished schools and hospitals needed saving from themselves by greater market and financial discipline. Nothing, or nothing very much, was to be said about Europe, crime, tax, and immigration – until, that is, the Tory 'brand' had been 'decontaminated' and the Party had earned 'permission to be heard' by those who'd grown used to thinking of the Conservatives as 'the nasty party'. It could then begin to hum some of the old tunes as well as the new ones. Handled in a self-consciously 'reasonable' and 'moderate' manner, tried and trusted vote-winners like immigration and law and order were brought back into the mix to produce a balanced offer with something in it both for middle-class liberals who had defected either to Blair or to the Lib Dems and for working-class traditionalists.

After rebalancing the Conservative offer in this way and thereby frightening Brown off holding an early autumn election in 2007, Cameron carried on talking tender as well as tough, refusing to heed the advice from the Tory-supporting press that he stop shilly-shallying and plump for the populist and Thatcherite agenda they continued to favour but which did his predecessors so little good.

Cameron was also prepared to risk accusations of high-handedness from within the Party. His apparent firmness over the MPs' expenses scandal, his willingness to demote colleagues who got him into trouble with the Party, with the country or the press, and his decision to pass responsibility for the Party's media operation from an old chum to a former tabloid editor suggested to many Tories that their leader's judgement and ruthlessness more than made up for his lack of experience. The downside of this, and of his near total grip on CCHQ (formerly Central Office) and his tendency to surround himself with a conclave of the like-minded (and similarly wealthy), was a degree of internal tension. But the latter was ultimately insufficient to outweigh the gratitude of most of the Party for the double-digit poll leads it had begun to clock up. These began to narrow as the election grew nearer, possibly because the resultant complacency led the leadership to reveal rather more of its intention to cut spending than was wise. But members from top to bottom hoped that the cushion they appeared to have (along with the fact that the massive amount of cash Cameron had helped to raise was being more efficiently distributed by Michael Ashcroft's 'target seats' team in CCHQ) would be enough to overcome an electoral system so 'biased' against the Conservatives that they would need a swing of around eight per cent to win an overall majority. In the end, Labour's ability, even as it went down to a dreadful defeat, to play on widespread fears that the Conservative Party had not changed as much as its leader claimed, plus Nick Clegg's headline-hogging performance in the televised leaders' debates, denied Cameron that majority. However, the fact that he came as close as he did, plus his willingness to gamble on a coalition with the Lib Dems, and the advantageous deal he made in negotiating it, surely means Cameron must rank as one of the Conservative Party's most impressive leaders of the opposition.

Conclusion

What happened to the Tories in opposition between 1997 and 2005 should make us wary of swallowing whole the idea that the Party's overriding goal is power. One thing Margaret Thatcher was determined to do was to make the Conservatives' ideology more explicit: knowing where they stood, why they stood there, and not being afraid to admit it, she reasoned, would motivate the Party when in opposition and would prevent it from being blown off course once in government. She was right, but there was a flip-side, a price paid by those who followed her as Tory leader. The politics of power is different from the politics of support. It may not be completely honest, nor even particularly democratic, but what a party actually does in office need bear only a passing resemblance to what it claims it wants to do in opposition.

The traditional recipe for recovering power is more easily written down than followed: it represents the what, not the how. The latter, the Tory experience between 1945 and 2010 suggests, can only be tackled after, firstly, acknowledging the scale and the scope of public disillusion with what you as a party have done and become in government and, secondly, by recognising that, in opposition, you are a price-taker rather than a price-maker. Deprived of the opportunity to implement policies that deliver the goods to key sections of the electorate, and having used up whatever chance you may have had of securing a long-term shift in public perceptions, you have to go with the grain rather than with your gut. Impressionism or pointillism: both will do – although the former seems to make for a significantly better (and therefore longer) experience in government. In opposition, however, the most important thing is to see voters as they are, not how you would like them to be.

6. Lessons for a Leader: Labour in Opposition

Greg Rosen

Greg Rosen is a Visiting Fellow in the Department of Politics at Goldsmiths, University of London and Chair of the Labour History Group. He is a political columnist for The Scotsman *and a former Vice-Chair of the Fabian Society. His previous books on history and public policy include* Serving the People *(Mutuo, 2007),* Old Labour to New *(Politico's, 2005), and* The Dictionary of Labour Biography *(Politico's, 2001).*

The Labour Party has spent far more of its history in opposition than in government. Unkind observers might suggest, given it has had so much practice, that it ought to be quite good at it. But Labour has spent so much time in opposition simply because it has not got better at it.

Why should this be the case? And what must Labour learn from its history to use opposition as a springboard, to emerge a renewed and rejuvenated Labour government at the next election?

Ed Miliband has his work cut out. Labour's vote share at the 2010 election was worse than at any time since 1931 (with the exception of 1983). The strength of its parliamentary position, though welcome, is deceptive.

The many talented new Labour MPs who have just won seats should not believe that coalition mistakes will result in an easy election win for Labour. For them simply to await the inevitable collapse of the Cameron–Clegg government might lead to a worse defeat than in 2010.

So, how can the Labour Party stay out of the political shadows? First, there are the lessons in what not to do. Following the fall of almost every previous Labour government, Labour has allowed itself to indulge in energetic bouts of fratricide. This was the case following Labour's defeat in 1931, after 1951, after 1970 and 1979. The worse the infighting, the longer Labour remained out of power. There has been only one exception: Labour's brief minority government of 1924, where, united in opposition, the Party returned to government at the next election.

Any government makes mistakes; some of commission, others of omission. It is always convenient to blame the unpopularity of a defeated government wholly on the personal failings of its leader. But politics is a team game and it would be foolish for Labour to repeat the mistakes of the early 1970s when the Party held Harold Wilson responsible for all its woes, or 1979/80 when defeated left-wing Labour MPs blamed leader Jim Callaghan. In fact, it was Callaghan's personal popularity with voters that had done most to buoy the Labour vote – it was Tony Benn and his allies with whom most voters felt out of step. While it is a convenient alibi for Ed Miliband's Labour Party to blame defeat in 2010 on Gordon Brown's personality – or indeed on 'Iraq', 'New Labour spin' or other 'alibi-issues', (if responsibility is to be shouldered, the new leadership can point the finger of blame at others) – it would be a mistake not to recognise the wider causes. It would also be a mistake not to reflect on Labour's poll ratings since May 2010, which have not risen much above the levels of an unpopular coalition, despite the absence of Brown, and despite the presence of a new leader.

The reasons for electoral defeat are often both more complex and more opaque – hence the opportunity for infighting among Party activists over competing ways of reading the political tea leaves. After 1979, for example, while moderates like Denis Healey, Merlyn Rees, John Smith and Roy Hattersley were clear in blaming the Winter of Discontent and Tony Benn's advocacy of more left-wing positions for undermining government credibility, those around Benn argued the opposite, insisting that the government had betrayed its supporters. Tony Benn and his allies foisted a more left-wing and statist manifesto on Labour for the following election and in doing so condemned Labour to its worst defeat since 1931.

Ironically, given the enthusiasm for 'debate' at that time, the arguments over policy changed few minds. It is hard to find many votes at Labour conferences that were changed by weight of argument. More often delegates arrived with pre-determined views and chose to listen to those who would validate, rather than challenge, their preconceptions. Many of the greatest conference speeches by Labour opposition leaders achieved little beyond their own rhetorical brilliance.

Hugh Gaitskell (Labour's leader from 1956 until his unexpected death in 1963) is perhaps best remembered for his pledge at the 1960 annual conference to 'fight and fight and fight again to save the party we love' from those trade union leaders whose block votes were committing the Party to support unilateral nuclear disarmament, a stance likely to lose Labour the next election. It was a speech made knowingly in defeat. There was never the slightest chance of his words actually persuading the trade union leaders to change their minds and support their leader. Gaitskell made his speech against a backdrop of intense factional infighting between the left- and right-wings of the Labour Party – infighting that had been a contributory factor to all three preceding Labour election defeats (in 1951, 1955 and 1959).

It was only the scale of Labour's defeat at the 1983 general election that forced some hitherto Bennites to realise that even if they supported Benn's policies, the electorate would not. This realisation split the 'left' into 'hard' (those who remained true to Benn's position) and 'soft' (those who supported Neil Kinnock in revising Labour's policies to reach an accommodation with the electorate). The 'hard-left' remain with Labour to this day in the form of the Campaign Group of Labour MPs, and their analysis of Labour's political position remains just as electorally incredible as it was in 1983.

Too often, Labour's behaviour in opposition has been determined by the belief of some activists that they can foist electorally unacceptable policies upon the Labour Party without consequence. They assume that the electorate's prospective disenchantment with a Conservative government will simply swing the electoral pendulum and propel Labour back into government. This was the tragedy of those who placed their devotion to the cause of unilateral nuclear disarmament above their commitment to the interests of those voters who depended on an electable Labour government.

Another mistake previous Labour oppositions have made is to behave like an ossified version of their previous incarnation in government. There is always the temptation for those who have held ministerial office to regard the future as a place in which they must defend their own political past. Labour should defend its achievements. But it needs to learn not to become the prisoner of the decisions of ex-ministers. This is all the more important following the defeat of a government that has been in office for a long time.

Some previous Labour leaders have struggled to define themselves as leader because of the strength of their pre-existing public persona. Thus, Neil Kinnock's public image as an outspoken enthusiast for policies such as unilateral nuclear disarmament, a policy to which a substantial majority of the electorate were antipathetic, made it almost impossible for him to lead Labour to victory. When he led the reforms of Labour's policies during the late 1980s, it was his reputation within the Party as a principled left-wing socialist that helped win the trust of those Party activists, who needed to vote for policy change contrary to their own preferences and instincts.

Kinnock was torn. Having changed Labour's policies, he had to persuade the public that he could be trusted to implement the newly voter-friendly programme. To achieve the changes, Kinnock felt compelled to pursue a gradualist 'softly-softly' approach. 'Until as late as 1991,' Kinnock later recalled, 'there was always a significant risk that any progressive lunge that was too big or too quick could have fractured the developing consensus and retarded the whole operation of reform and change.' But to convince the public that Labour really had changed he would have had to denounce the old policy positions, something which it was feared, probably correctly, would inflame many of the soft left who were unhappy enough at the policy shifts. And what, at any rate, did such profound changes of mind say about Kinnock's own judgement? For his admirers it was precisely these changes of mind that showed his strength of judgement; but for his enemies in the Conservative press – and he had many – they showed either his lack of judgement (his original views were bogus) or his opportunism (having abandoned them).

Michael Foot was even less fortunate as leader. His commitment to CND was not something on which he could credibly compromise. Like Kinnock, whose mentor he was, Michael Foot was a political giant whose talents and brilliance shone above most other politicians of his generation. Unlike Kinnock, Foot became leader in the autumn of his political life. He had fulfilled many roles with skill and success. Party leader proved not to be one to which his talents were best suited and he was old enough to tell his detractors that he was not prepared to be anything other than himself. On issues like the 'right-to-buy' council houses, Foot failed to prevent Labour from retreating into an 'oppositionalist' stance to the new government which proved, like the Venus fly trap, to be initially attractive but politically fatal. Instead of attacking the gaping flaws in the policy, namely the failure to structure it so that new social housing would be built to replace that sold, Labour found itself opposing the very principle of voters buying their own homes. And this even though it was a Labour Housing Minister, Bob Mellish, who had come up with the idea a decade before.

Clement Attlee was comparatively unknown when he became leader in 1935. He managed to overcome his lack of definition as an opposition leader by serving as deputy Prime Minister through five years of war. Moreover he was lucky to be able to field a talented team of strong personalities whom he was able to balance, enabling him to paint himself successfully against them as a kind of 'anti-personality'.

Harold Wilson and Tony Blair were Labour's two most effective opposition leaders. Both succeeded in defining themselves early and on their own terms. It is clear that David Cameron drew lessons from Blair's success. Cameron's most effective tactic as opposition leader was to take an issue of public resonance, address it in plain English, and adopt a stance. He embraced a policy which, while not necessarily providing a holistic solution, nevertheless was both practical and symbolic. In this, he was clearly influenced both by the American 'values' school of political campaigning beloved of Republican right-wingers and by the 'pledges', such as to 'get 250,000 under-25 year-olds off benefit and into work by using money from a windfall levy on the privatised utilities', at the heart of Labour's successful election campaign in 1997.

While learning from past Labour oppositions what not to do, Ed Miliband will also need to clarify what he *should* do. But whatever he decides, he will need to act quickly, for the history of previous Labour opposition leaders suggests that those who fail to define themselves early on their own terms are defined by their opponents. Arguably, if Ed Miliband waits until the conclusions of Labour's policy review before seeking to define himself in the public mind, he will have left it too late to win the next election.

Ed Miliband is less well known to voters than most previous Labour opposition leaders such as Neil Kinnock, Michael Foot, John Smith and Hugh Gaitskell. In this respect he enjoys the distinguished company of two of Labour's most successful opposition leaders, Clement Attlee and Tony Blair. Like them, he has the opportunity to use a relatively blank canvas to his advantage.

For most voters, who engage less and less with the great political rituals of the annual Party Conference circus, politics is less about vision and speeches and more about their experience of public services and the human stories that are the focus of media attention.

Tony Blair in opposition understood this. As shadow Home Secretary he spoke for the nation after the appalling murder of toddler Jamie Bulger. Blair's succinct encapsulation of the need for a Labour government to be both 'tough on crime and tough on the causes of crime' inspired voter confidence and both drew a line under Labour's 1980s' 'soft on crime' image and challenged the failure of the Tories' tough rhetoric to tackle the real problems of crime in society.

Learning this lesson from Blair, David Cameron in opposition was clever to pick out clear positions on what his strategists deemed 'defining issues' and explain how he would tackle them. His solutions were often ropey. For instance he proposed a 'marriage tax-break' to combat the problem of family breakdown, and though the details were insufficiently credible to withstand media scrutiny, the concepts were superficially coherent. Cameron had done more than simply pledge to reduce family breakdown by an arbitrary long-term target date.

Ed Miliband will need to learn these lessons. By 2005, Labour had got lost in a rhetorical cul-de-sac of vague phrases like 'your community safer' and 'your children with the best start'. In 2010, pledges were clearer (and had verbs), though they nevertheless failed to address some of the deeper concerns voters had about the government.

Now the central defining issue of the first two years of the coalition is the spending review. The coalition will continue to seek to undermine potential voter confidence and trust in Ed Miliband, to paint him as 'evasive' and a 'risk' for voters, through the prism of the spending review and the public debate around 'cuts', and by taking positions on issues and challenging Miliband to oppose or concede. And if he opposes, the coalition will demand an alternative policy.

Cleverly, the coalition has already used Labour's failure to hold a comprehensive spending review before the election as an opportunity to pretend that Labour's critique of government cuts is somehow bogus. It will simply not wash with the electorate for Labour to claim that because it is not in government it does not need to offer a view on how the deficit should best be reduced, beyond saying that it would have cut less and later. Labour was right not to cost a comprehensive alternative spending review to the coalition in October 2010. But its public credibility would benefit from laying out some symbolic alternatives to the coalition's specific plans, and give examples to show how a Labour government would have acted, and would act, differently. But as 2011 progresses, and the cuts begin to bite there is still scope for Labour to use them to define itself.

Many voters have yet to fully grasp the scale of the coalition's cuts agenda – and the popularity of the coalition is likely to dip as that sinks in. It is far from clear, however, whether that unpopularity will benefit Labour, or whether votes will give the benefit of the doubt to the coalition's claim that all the cuts are required to address to deficit.

To win the next election, Ed Miliband will need to define himself quickly – and in the right way. And that requires an understanding of the deeper underlying reasons, beyond the

Iraq war, for Labour's decline in the polls since the heady days of 1997 and 2001.

In opposition, Labour has an opportunity to 'reconnect' with its roots; indeed with its very reason for being. While much of Labour's purpose endures, its policies and priorities must necessarily evolve as society changes. Unless these policies are rooted in the lives and aspirations of sufficient voters, electoral victory will prove elusive.

To escape opposition, it will not be enough for Labour to assemble an electoral coalition of the 'progressive' middle classes, non-military public sector employees, the unemployed, the marginalised and the 'vulnerable'. For a start, the truly 'vulnerable' tend not to vote, and many others defined as such might actually vote Conservative.

This raises the question: who does Labour speak for? Is it Party activists, members or wider voters? To what extent is it and should it be union leaders, activists and members? In the past, this question had a simpler answer. Originally, most Labour voters, activists and members were members of affiliated trade unions whose membership was comprised primarily of private-sector employees. Indeed, until 1918 there were no individual Labour Party members, only those who were members through their unions, and those unions, representing miners, steelworkers, engineers, electricians, train drivers, boilermakers, road haulage drivers and dockers, represented the aspirational skilled and semi-skilled British blue-collar workforce. White-collar union members, such as teachers, could join as individual members only from the 1920s, and most of their unions were never affiliated to the Labour Party.

To this day, prominent unions such as Mark Serwotka's PCS civil service union and the National Union of Teachers remain non-affiliated. But while they are bigger than ever, and their memberships are considered by many Labour MPs to make up part of Labour's 'core vote', the more traditional Labour-affiliated unions have shrunk. Many of those representing workers in the private sector are pale shadows of their size in the 1970s, and many of the largest, including the old engineering and electrical unions representing skilled manufacturing workers are now part of UNITE, a mega union which considers itself as much a union representing the interests of its substantial public sector membership as it does the skilled blue-collar workers at car manufacturers such as Ford and Toyota.

Indeed, while the majority of public sector workers are now unionised, the majority of private-sector employees are no longer. This has had implications for the policy focus of the TUC as a whole, for whom the preservation of public sector jobs has become a far higher priority than issues such as pension provision for skilled and semi-skilled private-sector workers. The risk is that the interests of 'C2' workers in the private sector, whose votes are vital if Labour is to win an election, and for whom unions such as AMICUS (now subsumed within UNITE) once gave a voice, are neglected. They are part of the 'squeezed middle', recently highlighted by Liam Byrne and others. In decades past, the likes of Jim Callaghan and Herbert Morrison knew instinctively their aspirations, but no longer.

When Labour was in opposition during the 1970s and 1980s Terry Duffy, Gavin Laird and Bill Jordan of the old engineers' union, Bill Sirs of the steelworkers, and Frank Chapple and Eric Hammond of the electricians' and plumbers' were there to remind middle-class Labour MPs of the aspirations of the voters Labour needed to attract to win elections. The diminution of that voice in Labour's senior counsels has robbed the 'squeezed middle' of 'their' champions, and unbalanced Labour's internal policy debates.

Since the 1987 election defeat, having divested themselves of the electoral albatross of CND, Labour leaders have sought to give their party a sufficiently broad electoral appeal by uniting it around a vision of properly-funded, high-quality public services. This was at the heart of Labour's unsuccessful pitch to voters in 1992, and its highly successful election campaign in 1997. The key difference was that in 1992 Labour pledged openly to increase tax (particularly National Insurance) to pay for better services, whereas in 1997 Labour promised to improve services in a more fiscally restrained manner, explaining through its 'Five Pledges' how specific extra spending commitments were to be funded from savings elsewhere (e.g. funding smaller primary school class sizes by redeploying the money saved from axing the Assisted Places Scheme). Gordon Brown's insight, that the trust of the electorate to spend public money needed to be earned, was shrewd. It was, in Brown's much-parodied phrase, prudence with an (electoral) purpose. And it worked. Only after four successful and popular years in government did Brown judge that he had built sufficient support to raise National Insurance a penny to pay for greater NHS spending.

Gordon Brown's second great insight as shadow Chancellor showed the practical application of his historical expertise and was an attempt to address what he identified as being the most important prerequisite for the success of a Labour government. His great insight as opposition shadow Chancellor – which underpinned the idea of 'prudence with a purpose' – was that every previous Labour government had been derailed by an economic crisis (all save Ramsay MacDonald's brief first minority government of 1924 which had been derailed simply by its own lack of a Commons majority). None of these economic crises were of Labour's making. Some, like the unsustainably overvalued Pound Sterling inherited by Harold Wilson in 1964, were the legacy of Conservative economic mismanagement. Others, like the consequences of the 1973 oil price shock inherited by Wilson in 1974, of the Wall Street Crash inherited by Ramsay MacDonald in 1929, and of the Second World War inherited by Attlee in 1945, were global phenomena that happened to spill in Labour's lap. Each and every one of them had cracked the credibility of the Labour government of the day, and undermined its ability to invest in the better society it had promised.

For a Labour Party whose core electoral appeal was a vision of properly-funded high-quality 'collective' and universal public services, an economic crisis would force cuts and deferred spending which would torpedo 'New Labour' just as surely as it had previous Labour governments. Brown recognised that for voters to see that public investment in a better society would pay off required an economic climate conducive to that investment, and he set out to deliver it. His success, until the global economic crisis, was unparalleled – who now remembers shadow Chancellor Francis Maude's prediction during New Labour's first term in government of a 'Downturn made in Downing Street'?

But the very success of Brown's strategy has ironically exposed Labour's failure to think profoundly and creatively beyond 'tax and spend'. It highlighted the fact Brown's Labour had not fulfilled Peter Mandelson's professed credo that Labour needed to be not simply bigger spenders than the Conservatives but wiser spenders too; they needed to be in his words '..."effective state" social democrats, not simply "big state" social democrats...'

Essentially, while Gordon Brown's insight that a Labour government needed to avoid an economic crisis if it was to succeed was true, it was over-optimistic for Labour to assume that it would, in itself, guarantee its long-term success and popularity. While Labour could point out that many of the Conservative alternatives to Labour's plans implied even greater spending than Labour had undertaken (and given Conservative priorities to reduce costs, that amounted to a false prospectus) this amounted to little more than a tactic to distract attention from Labour's own lack of coherent thinking in this area.

Some might try to blame Brown entirely for Labour's

failure to develop a sufficiently effective plan for efficient government. But for all his rhetoric of public service reform, Tony Blair failed to focus on the effectiveness of his government's spending decisions either. The much-vaunted 'delivery unit' played a necessary role in facilitating many of the successes that the government enjoyed, but it was not in itself sufficient to spread successful 'delivery' across government. As Blair's second term progressed, mundanities of public sector procurement had less and less appeal, and Blair became far more interested in and focused on foreign policy. By 2006, even before Brown took over as Prime Minister, voters were becoming increasingly concerned at the effectiveness of government at spending their money.

Post-2010, voters care just as much about improving public services as they did in 1997. But they also believe it to be necessary to close the deficit. And at the 2010 election too few were prepared to trust the job to Labour for the fundamental reason that they had lost confidence in the competence of Labour to best invest public money in the public service improvements that they still support – not that the election result showed any great trust in the Conservatives to do a better job. Under William Hague's leadership the Tories' 'waste' argument – that Labour's extra spending was being 'wasted' – failed to resonate with voters. A decade later, too many voters had had their own experiences of inadequately managed public projects to dismiss Tory claims that Labour was insufficiently prudent in its deployment of public money. To win the next election on the basis of the 1992/97 appeal – better funded public services – Ed Miliband will need to convince voters that Labour can be trusted to spend their money better, not only than the Conservatives, but also than the last Labour government.

Anthony Crosland famously sought to focus the Labour Party on the difference between 'ends' and 'means', emphasising that the latter should be considered flexibly, and should not become ends in themselves. He was right to do so, and in opposition, Labour has too often been tempted to elevate the 'means' considered fashionable at any given time (be that central planning or nationalised state ownership) into a desirable end in itself. Tony Blair sought to revive and renew Crosland's dictum in his own belief that 'what matters is what works' and the importance of 'evidence-based policymaking'. He never, however, answered the question of what does 'work' best, in part because the 'evidence' for much public policy is opaque and correlative, rather than causal. It is often impossible to 'prove' what 'works' best, because the control experiments necessary to provide conclusive proof are impossible to conduct in the real world. This is actually exacerbated when ministers have an army of civil service advisers competing to offer their own interpretations of the 'evidence'.

The longer governments remain in office, the more they come to rely on their civil servants for detailed policy-making. A couple of Special Advisers in a government department of thousands can do little to alter that fact. And too few think tanks have the primary research capacity, or indeed the access to confidential government statistics, to offer sufficient alternative expertise.

This has two implications. Firstly that ministerial decisions, advised by an army of civil servants and the best 'evidence' available, may nevertheless have been wrong-headed, and for ex-ministers now in opposition to defend their record in the face of public perception of mistakes may be simply to compound their misjudgements.

Secondly, aware of the meagre calibre of policy-making resources their party has been able to call upon in opposition (thanks to Short Money and the proliferation of think tanks since the 1980s it is better now than ever it was in the past) Labour shadow ministers have tended to confine their thinking to what the next Labour government 'should' or 'must' seek to do, leaving the 'how' question to those clever civil servants and their libraries of evidence to work out once Labour returns to government. After all if the ends are more important than the means, and 'what matters is what works', that can illusorily appear to be the best approach.

But it is wrong, for unless the ends are attainable, it is no good simply willing them with targets and goals. It is all very well to aspire to 'progressive' goals, but targets in themselves are little use without an effective, workable strategy to achieve them. It will not be enough for Labour 'policy wonks' to urge action when the real question is not so much whether 'something should be done' but how?

Ed Miliband will need to be more interested in the 'how' question than were his predecessors. The greatest risk for Labour in opposition post-2010 is that there will be a paucity of ideas for *how* a future Labour government can do a better job than the one that was defeated at the last election. Every Labour government has aspired to persuade voters to trust it to help secure better public services. But while voters do not doubt the aspiration, Labour's faith in opposition that the civil service would sort out the 'delivery' bit on ministers' behalf means public perceptions of Labour's effectiveness in government were tarred by weaknesses in Whitehall.

Moreover, the competence and effectiveness of Labour in government was undermined by the failure of ministers to resolve the inherent conflicts and contradictions within and between policies. For example, on a broad level, a 'needs-based' allocation of social housing inevitably directs resources to those with the largest families, causing resentment amongst those who might have been waiting longer, or who may have been working hard and paying into the welfare system to a greater extent than those who benefit most from it.

Labour's perceived fitness to govern was undermined by an inability or unwillingness by ministers to resolve such conflicting priorities. 'To govern is to choose', as Pierre Mendes-France, perhaps the greatest premier of the French Fourth Republic, observed, and opposition allows a party the luxury of avoiding such choices. But it is foolish to luxuriate in such irresponsibility while retaining aspirations to power.

The Brown government's handling of the 'Gurkha issue' in the spring of 2009 is just one example of the difficulty Labour had when in office resolving conflicting priorities in line with its principles, in this case its belief in 'fairness'. In the media, Labour's opposition to allowing Gurkhas to settle in the UK, irrespective of whether they had fought and been injured in the defence of the UK, was juxtaposed with headlines describing the small fortune in legal aid and state benefits accumulated by Abu Qatada and other foreign terror-supporting Islamist militants whom the Labour government desired, yet failed, to deport.

Underpinning Labour's fairness agenda was a significant investment in public service interventions by the Blair and Brown governments designed to support the most vulnerable in society. It does not come cheap. But the evidence-base used by government suggests that policy and investment needs to be heavily targeted on the most difficult cases – or, in the preferred euphemism of our era, those 'hardest to reach' – for society as a whole to benefit. But when the effectiveness of that investment is called into question by such high-profile tragedies as the Baby P fiasco, voters question whether government (national or local), really can be trusted to make the best use of their money. Some have sought to argue that Haringey social services was underfunded and overstretched. But if that is the case when record sums have been invested in social services and local government, it begs the question of how much money would be sufficient to enable the current system of public services to operate competently, and how possible that will ever be? Unless Labour can inspire confidence in the competence of the machine of government, if it is seeking to persuade voters to believe in the ability of an 'active government' or indeed an 'enabling state' to make their lives better, it is all the more likely to lose an election.

Ed Miliband's job will not be any the easier for the fact Labour was born as an opposition party. Indeed, when the Party was formed, many of its putative supporters – men and women – were not even allowed the vote. Only after 1918 did Labour seriously entertain the possibility of aspiring to lead a government. And though Labour's structure and approach evolved over its first two decades, it never shed its origins as a 'bottom-up' party of protest and influence, as opposed to a party of governmental responsibility and power, as the Conservative Party and its predecessors have always been.

Sharpened as it was by the events of 1931, Labour retains a cultural predisposition to fear 'betrayal' in government by its leadership. For this reason, Labour activists have spent a far greater proportion of their time than activists in other parties seeking to prescribe policy goals for their leaders and devise ways to force those same leaders to realise them. Moreover, because responsibility for Labour failures in government are all too often ascribed by activists to having been a failure of socialist willpower by the leadership, little if any time is spent in opposition analysing whether the prescribed policies would either achieve the desired goal or are practical and possible. Instead, focus is placed on devising new and more painful sanctions for errant MPs and leaders should the next time Labour be in government they again encounter a failure of will. But if Labour fails next time it is less likely to be a failure of 'will' than a failure of 'how'.

To be a successful opposition leader, Ed Miliband needs to draw on the lessons of history. He must minimise party infighting, define himself early, in the context of salient public issues, and do so in a way that convinces the electorate that he not only shares their aspirations, but has a workable plan to realise them. He will also need to remember not just how much Labour has been shaped by its history, but how much it has changed, and address the 'new disconnect' between Labour's representative institutions and the 'squeezed middle', whose support Labour needs to secure, and which includes the same skilled private-sector workers who were the founders of the Labour Party more than a century ago.

7. Ignored, Irresponsible and Irrelevant?: Opposition MPs in the House of Commons

Philip Cowley and Mark Stuart

Philip Cowley is Professor of Parliamentary Government at the University of Nottingham. His most recent book (with Dennis Kavanagh) is The British General Election of 2010 *(Palgrave, 2010). Mark Stuart teaches Politics at both Nottingham and Hull Universities, helps to run the revolts website (www. revolts.co.uk) and has written biographies of Douglas Hurd and John Smith.*

The political scientist Tony King once described British politics as 'over-the-shoulder politics'. What matters to a government minister in the House of Commons is not the opposition of the people sitting across the Chamber from him or her; what matters most is the opposition from those who sit behind. 'One discounts the disapproval of the other party,' he wrote, 'the disapproval of one's own is harder to bear.'[1] Indeed, this is a point which government ministers need to understand to avoid getting into difficulties. But it is also one that opposition MPs need to understand to avoid continual disappointment and frustration. For the most part, their lot is to watch, impotently, as the government wins vote after vote. Yet at the same time, opposition does have its advantages, which they can use to make life a little more bearable.

1. A. King, 'The Implications of one-party government', in A. King et al, *Britain At The Polls, 1992*, Chatham, NJ (Chatham House, 1993)

*

One of the enduring myths of British politics is that it is excessively adversarial: that the political parties routinely oppose everything each other does. Yet beneath the bluster, they don't disagree with each other half as much as is usually implied – or half as much as they make out.

Richard Rose demonstrated this as far back as 1980 by examining the way that the official opposition voted on Bills' Second Reading (the vote on the principle of the Bill) and/or Third Reading (the vote on the Bill as finally constituted). Rose showed that, despite all the talk of conflict and divisions, the opposition rarely voted against more than a quarter of government Bills.[2] Even at the height of adversarial politics between 1979 and 1983, with the gulf between the two parties at its widest since the Second World War, the official opposition, then Labour, voted against just over a third of the Thatcher government's legislation at Second or Third Reading.[3]

In the last parliament some four-fifths of government legislation was allowed through without the official opposition calling a vote at Second or Third Reading. The Tory frontbench contested the principle of just thirty-five government Bills out of a possible 171. This was significantly down on the 32 per cent average for the whole of the 2001 parliament, which was itself down on the 41 per cent in the 1997 parliament (see Table 1 below). As the New Labour era progressed, fewer and fewer government Bills were contested by the official opposition. This downward trend began before David Cameron became Conservative Party leader, although it became much more noticeable under his leadership.

---

2. R. Rose, *Do Parties Make A Difference?* (Macmillan, 1980)
3. D. Van Mechelen and R. Rose, *Patterns of Parliamentary Legislation* (Gower, 1986)

1. Conservative contestation of government legislation, 1997–2010

Parliament	Government Bills	Bills contested by Conservative frontbench	As % of government Bills
1997–2001	154	63	41
2001–2005	144	46	32
2005–2010)	171	35	20

Note: The figures show the Bills on which the Conservative frontbench chose to divide the House at Second and/or Third Reading. They exclude government Bills where the Conservative Parliamentary Party had free votes, but include Reasoned Amendments on Second or Third Reading.

At one point, when the Conservatives had failed to vote against the principle of a government Bill for a full six months, the Conservative explanation was that they were not prepared to fall for Gordon Brown's tricks. ('He wants to manoeuvre us into a position where we are seen to be voting against motherhood and apple pie. So rather than vote against the Bill as a whole we try to change it later,' they said.) There were, of course, plenty of occasions when the Conservatives did precisely that: not opposing at Second or Third Reading, but later attempting to amend legislation during Committee or Report stage. Yet there was clearly something going on. The data clearly shows a parliament-by-parliament decline in the propensity of the opposition to object to the principle of government legislation. William Hague's Conservative Party voted against the principle of about two out of every five Bills. Under Iain Duncan Smith and Michael Howard, that fell slightly, to just under one in three. But under David Cameron it had fallen yet further, down to just one of every five pieces of government legislation.

The Conservative explanation, however, does point to a truth about parliamentary voting. It has a symbolic purpose:

divisions are about putting on record the Party's stance on an issue. In many ways, this symbolic purpose is the most important; divisions are not called in order to discover a previously unknown outcome. Unless the Chamber is hung – as it was in the late-1970s or briefly in the mid-1990s – opposition MPs know that they are outnumbered, and the government will win. They therefore have just two hopes. The first is subterfuge. Occasionally, opposition whips will be able to pull off an ambush, massing their troops secretly whilst government MPs drift home, and then suddenly revealing them *en masse* for a vote. In February 1999, during the passage of the Rating (Valuation) Bill, opposition Conservative whips ordered their MPs to leave the Commons. Labour MPs followed. Then, five minutes later, the Tory MPs returned suddenly. A government with a majority of 179 scraped through by twenty-five votes. This tactic rarely works, but it can at least cause panic on the government's side of the House, and helps keeps their whips on their toes.

An opposition's other hope lies in rebellion, from pressure from over the minister's shoulder, on those occasions when there are enough government MPs willing to vote with the opposition to defeat the government. Their chances here have at least improved slightly. Although occasionally a government might amend or withdraw policy as a result of backbench opinion and pressure, no prime minister from 1945 until 1970 had been defeated in the Commons as a result of their own MPs defying their party whip (the handful of defeats that did occur were caused by poor organisation on the part of the whips or as a result of tactical manoeuvres by the opposition).[4] Since then, every prime minister, from Heath to Brown, has been defeated at least once in the Commons as a result of their own MPs allying with the opposition.

---
4. P. Norton, *Dissension in the House of Commons, 1945–1974*, (Macmillan, 1975)

Yet for all that, Commons defeats remain rare. Apart from the period between 1974 and 1979 (when there were twenty-three defeats caused by the government's own backbenchers rebelling, along with thirty-six attributed to its minority status), every recent prime minister's Commons defeats can all be measured in single figures.[5] Tony Blair went two whole terms without suffering a single defeat in the Commons; in his third term, with a smaller majority, he went down to four defeats (two on pre-trial detention, two on religious hatred), but that represents four defeats out of more than 3,000 votes. Gordon Brown suffered two defeats (on the settlement rights of the Gurkhas and parliamentary standards).

Even on votes where there looks like the possibility of victory – when the press start to talk of 'concern' in the government whips' office and run profiles of 'key' rebels – the reality is that rebellions usually melt away, the would-be dissidents bought off by a series of concessions and compromises, by their desire not to harm their own government and (in some cases) by the lure of self-advancement. The government whips have, in different ways, far more resources than any putative rebellion, and as a result usually win.

Opposition MPs therefore need to get used to watching the government emerge victorious in vote after vote. At the time of writing, the coalition is undefeated in the Commons. Its first six months have seen an unprecedented level of dissent amongst government MPs, but no defeats. At over eighty, the combined Con–Lib Dem Commons majority is larger than many people realise. It is not quite of landslide proportions, but is larger than the majorities enjoyed by Winston Churchill after 1945, Anthony Eden, Harold Wilson (1966–70 excepted), Edward Heath, James Callaghan, Margaret Thatcher (in her first term), John Major (after 1992), as well as Tony Blair and Gordon

---

5. P. Norton, *Dissension in the House of Commons, 1974–1979* (Clarendon Press, 1980) p. 439

Brown in Labour's third term. As that list indicates, smaller majorities have proved perfectly sufficient to last for full four- or five-year terms, and (in most cases) without the government suffering from routine defeats. Moreover, the fact that the government's rebellions are coming from both sides of the coalition offers them some protection, as it is difficult to find issues on which both flanks – the right of the Conservatives and the left of the Lib Dems – will coalesce. This is especially true of the coalition's left flank. Almost 40 per cent of Lib Dem MPs are in government – either as ministers or Parliamentary Private Secretaries (PPSs). That leaves around thirty-five Liberal Democrat backbenchers at any one time. Therefore, even if every Lib Dem backbencher votes against the government, it still wins. On the right of the coalition, there are many more disgruntled right-wing Conservative MPs, but they are much less likely to be able to find an issue on which they will be able to vote with the Labour opposition. This explains why, despite the string of rebellions, until the student fees vote in December 2010 the government's majority had not fallen below fifty-one, and why even an issue as toxic as that could only reduce it to a reasonably comfortable twenty-one. This is not to say that an issue will not come along on which the left and the right of the coalition can combine (there is always the potential for an issue in which the different wings of the government object for different reasons) but it will be harder than it looks on paper.

So opposition MPs need to get used to night after night of trooping through the lobbies, fuelled by the righteousness of their stance and by the power of their arguments, convinced that only a fool or a knave could vote with the government – only to lose heavily. They need to realise, and realise early on, that whilst arguments may be won, votes will almost certainly be lost.

*

Yet there are advantages to being in opposition. In July 2010 the government moved a draft order to keep the 28-day pre-charge detention for suspected terrorists in place for six months, pending a broader review of its anti-terrorism measures. The Labour frontbench line was to support the government in the aye lobby, but out of just sixty Labour MPs who voted no fewer than thirty voted against, the Party splitting precisely in half. Ten of the Labour rebels who voted against the order were members of the 2010 intake of MPs, five of them ethnic minority Members. Had this split occurred when Labour was in government, it would have been front-page news. But it was barely reported.

Whilst no one likes to be ignored, it can occasionally be useful, especially if your party is divided over an issue. The truth is that the media report rebellions by government MPs, but they ignore them when they involve opposition MPs. This is not a political get out of jail free card. It is possible to so spectacularly cock things up that even the media notice an opposition split. Iain Duncan Smith's Conservatives managed this in November 2002, when they whipped against allowing unmarried couples (including homosexual couples) to adopt. A relatively small rebellion followed on what became dubbed 'gay adoption', but one in which Michael Portillo defied the whip. All the attention was on Portillo, and on divisions within the Party.[6] Nick Clegg and the Liberal Democrats managed something similar over the Lisbon ratification in March 2008, when maladroit handling of the issue caused a nasty party split over the issue of a referendum on the Treaty. The Party suffered a large backbench revolt and frontbench resignations (along with a bizarre intra-party split between its positions in the two Chambers of Parliament).[7]

---
6. P. Cowley, *The Rebels* (Politico's, 2005) pp. 275–6
7. P. Cowley and M. Stuart, 'Where has all the trouble gone? British intra-party

But for the most part, no one cares what opposition MPs do. The best example of this came during John Major's premiership. For much of the period from 1992, the media focused with searing intensity on the divisions within Major's Parliamentary Party and the term 'Conservative Party unity' became an oxymoron. The Conservatives lost their reputation for unity (a reputation they had long enjoyed), with the blame for this laid largely at the feet of the Party's MPs. Yet during the 1992 parliament it was Labour MPs, not Conservatives, who had been the most rebellious. Even over Europe – the issue that so damaged the Major government – it was Labour MPs who were the most divided.[8] But almost no one noticed or cared.

Opposition also allows whips to duck issues entirely, by granting free votes on topics. Government can do this too – on issues such as abortion or hunting. But on other issues the government is less able collectively to shrug its shoulders and abdicate responsibility. Opposition can, and it often proves a useful way of avoiding damaging splits within the party. Iain Duncan Smith, for example, would have been well advised not to have whipped the vote on gay adoption. A free vote on the same subject – with the same divisions – would not have produced anywhere near the same problems. Indeed, David Cameron proved this when in opposition in March 2007, he allowed a free vote over the Draft Equality Act (Sexual Orientation) Regulations, another measure dealing with 'gay adoption'. Faced with a thoroughly divided Party, Cameron granted his troops a free vote. Twenty-nine Conservatives, including Cameron, George Osborne and the bulk of the shadow Cabinet voted for the measure, while eighty-five mostly Tory backbenchers voted against. The Conservative

---

parliamentary divisions during the Lisbon ratification', *British Politics*, 2010
8. P. Cowley and P. Norton with M. Stuart and M. Bailey, *Blair's Bastards: discontent within the Parliamentary Labour Party*. Research Paper in Legislative Studies 1/96 (University of Hull Centre for Legislative Studies, 1996)

leader had therefore voted in a different direction to the majority of his party, but almost no one criticised him for it.

A more recent example came in October 2010 with an amendment to the Parliamentary Voting System and Constituencies Bill that would have extended the franchise to 16- and 17-year-olds in the AV referendum. The government had to take a position on the issue (and whipped against). The opposition did not. Faced with a divided Parliamentary Party – the bulk of the Labour Party was in favour of the move, although a good number of the old guard of former ministers were thoroughly opposed to the idea (sensible people that they are) – a free vote was given. In the event, 183 Labour MPs voted for and eleven against, and all views were accommodated within the Party, without any rancour.

*

Part of opposition is taking the fight to the enemy. Think of the most difficult parliamentary battle of the last fifty years: the battle over the ratification of the Maastricht Treaty. It took more than a year of parliamentary debate, marked by continuous backbench dissent on the part of Conservative MPs. Tristan Garel-Jones, the Minister of State at the Foreign Office at the time, recalls the Conservative Parliamentary Party as 'bleeding to death for over a year'.[9]

Yet this was an issue on which the Labour frontbench officially supported the government. They welcomed the Maastricht Treaty, and would have signed it too; despite the divisions within Labour's ranks, there was an overwhelming majority in the House for the treaty. Its ratification should have been simple and painless. Yet despite the Labour leader, John Smith, being avowedly pro-European, he was prepared to use almost any parliamentary device available to drag the process out, finding areas where his party could disagree with

---

9. M. Stuart, *Douglas Hurd* (Mainstream, 1998) p. 299

the government, highlighting the Conservative divisions. It was not, he felt, the opposition's job to make life easy for the government; Labour's aim was to embarrass it, not to bring down the Treaty.

Aided by two newly elected MPs, Stephen Byers and Geoff Hoon, Smith's shadow Europe Minister George Robertson, plotted a series of parliamentary traps. They would put down 'probing amendments', raising an issue for debate, but then not pressing it to a vote. They would vote against allowing the government to move its Business Motion at 10p.m., which would have allowed it to carry on debating the Bill until the small hours of the morning, therefore dragging out debate over many more days. Their most successful ruse was originally known as Amendment 27 – and became known as the 'ticking time bomb' – which said that the treaty could only be ratified if the House passed a motion on the Social Chapter. This allied Labour MPs (who objected to the government's opt-out from the Social Chapter of the Treaty) with Conservative Eurosceptics (who hated the Social Chapter, but thought this was a way of blocking the Treaty). In July 1993 this led to a government defeat, and to John Major having to resort to a vote of confidence in order to get the measure through.

So proud was Robertson of his Maastricht campaign that he had a limited edition commemorative mug produced. Labour's guerrilla tactics meant that ministers were deprived of time for the other workings of government. As Robertson had argued in front of the PLP a few months before: 'Every day that is spent on this legislation is a day which is not spent on some other item in their legislative programme.'[10] The authority of the government drained away and morale in the PLP – desperately low after Labour's fourth successive election defeat – was restored.

---

10. Minutes of the Party meeting held on 18 February 1993 at 6p.m. in Committee Room 11

*

Opposition MPs can show their fighting qualities in many other ways, with or without the support of their frontbench. During the first Blair government, for example, a small group of Conservative backbench MPs, loosely organised around two former ministers, Eric Forth and David Maclean, began to engage in a parliamentary form of guerrilla warfare, which one of them likened to the behaviour of the French Resistance during the Second World War:

> When France was invaded, it was finished. Then two and a half thousand out of 40 million joined the *Maquis*. We can't defeat the government in votes, we can't defeat them in argument, since no one ever listens, but we can tie them down in the way that the *Maquis* tied down the Germans... it's only pot shots, but it's a form of opposition.[11]

They began by blocking Private Members' Bills, then moved on to object to otherwise non-contentious Bills, calling divisions and filibustering during their passage.[12] In July 1999, Forth and colleagues divided the House over nine consecutive motions and Statutory Instruments. Each vote took between 12–15 minutes, itself wasteful of government MPs' time, but the prospect of unexpected divisions would force the government whips to keep enough of their MPs in the precincts of the Commons to ensure victory, inconveniencing them yet further. Just as frustrating for Labour MPs were those occasions when Conservative MPs would keep the debate going into the early hours, only then *not* to call a vote, having kept hundreds of Labour MPs present, just in case.

---

11. This quote is taken from P. Cowley, *Revolts and Rebellions: Parliamentary Voting Under Blair* (Politico's, 2002) p. 198. The behaviour of Forth et al is summarised in pp. 197–204
12. See, for example, H. Marsh and D. Marsh, 'Tories in the Killing Fields', *Journal of Legislative Studies*, 2002

The exemplar of this behaviour was the Disqualifications Bill where opposition from Conservative backbenchers resulted in the deliberations of the Committee of the Whole House running from 5.43p.m. on 25 January 2000 to 7.19a.m. the following day. As a result, a whole day's business, including Prime Minister's Questions, was lost.

Many Labour MPs despaired of Forth's behaviour (which, of course, only encouraged him and his colleagues more). But some Labour MPs knew that they would have done the same, producing grudging admiration. During the 1970 parliament, a similar ginger group of Labour backbenchers had been set up by James Wellbeloved, which aimed, amongst other things, to 'knock a bit of stuffing out of the government backbenchers'.[13] During the late 1980s, with the PLP falling apart in organisational terms, and with MPs beset by reselection battles, two opposition MPs – Dennis Skinner and Bob Cryer – had similarly taken the fight to the Conservative government, by opposing legislation late into the night (which was why one long-serving Labour Member in the 1997 parliament described Eric Forth as 'Dennis Skinner in drag').

The point about such freelancing is not just that the MPs themselves would often enjoy it ('it gives me a purpose in life', said one, 'gets me up perkier in the morning'), but it was a way of causing the government difficulties without dirtying the hands of the frontbench. As Derek Foster, a former Labour Chief Whip ('with a PhD in opposition') admitted, he frequently encouraged his backbenchers: 'There were many times when I did not have complete control over my backbenchers. There were even more times when I pretended not to have control over them and colluded with them in frustrating the government of the day.'[14] Foster was opposition Chief Whip when the Labour opposition broke off links with the government for a period of five months in

---

13. P. Norton, *Dissension in the House of Commons 1945–1974*, p. 389
14. HC Deb 28 June 2001 c825

1993–94. There was no pairing for any purpose, and 'every possible parliamentary advantage would be exploited to disrupt the government's legislative programme' until further notice.[15] Night after night, Labour backbenchers kept two to three hundred Conservative MPs out of their beds.

The Labour backbencher Austin Mitchell once described Commons opposition as 'heckling the steamroller'. Faced with the reality of their irrelevance, it can be hard to keep opposition MPs in good spirits for long. Activity like this may not achieve anything substantive, but it plays a useful role in boosting morale, especially when a party has no serious prospect of returning to power for several years.

---

15. Minutes of the Parliamentary Labour Party meeting held on Thursday 9 December 1993 at 6p.m. in Committee Room 10

8. Voices in the Dark: The Opposition and the Media

Guy Black

Lord Black of Brentwood was Press Secretary and Director of Communications for Michael Howard as leader of the opposition from 2003–2005. He is now Executive Director of the Telegraph Media Group and became a member of the House of Lords in July 2010.

The job of dealing with the media in opposition is relentless, merciless and thankless. It consumes you eighteen hours a day – from the first headlines on *Today* to the evening paper review on Sky News – and three hundred and sixty-four days a year. (In truth, Christmas Eve, the one day in the year when no papers are produced for the next day and reporters are all rightly doing their shopping, is the only guaranteed day of quiet you have.) And much of the time – when the news is all about government – getting attention is like pushing water uphill.

But it is still an absolutely vital job. This is an age when political parties no longer have battalions of foot soldiers to spread the message directly through newsletters and canvassing, when party political broadcasts are few and far between and seldom watched, and when big advertising campaigns are too costly. Opposition parties will always have to rely in between elections – when debates are likely to now take centre stage – on the broadcast media, on newspapers and magazines, and increasingly on digital technology to get their message across and to attack the government. Professional media planning and execution is therefore integral to the role of opposition.

That said, all political parties when first thrust into the media permafrost that follows a general election defeat – and indeed for years afterwards – face a number of systemic difficulties in dealing with the media. It's worth identifying those, and I think there are six of them.

First, and wholly predictably, there is enormous imbalance in resources between the government communications machine and an opposition press office. Opposition parties face not just the political press and digital operations of their opponents, buoyed up by an election victory, but the weight of a government information machine whose job day in day out is to put over impartially and professionally the government's story, laud its achievements and help mitigate bad news. To counter that, an opposition, depleted and deflated in defeat, has tiny numbers of press officers in comparison. Even at the peak of activity before the 2005 general election, the Conservative press operation numbered fewer than forty dedicated and hard-working souls: but they faced a relentless barrage from all the information outlets the government had at its disposal.

Second, opposition parties often tend to spend much of their time soul-searching and navel-gazing. Hard-edged policies which attract media attention come only late on in a parliament, not least because oppositions are naturally anxious that eye-catching and popular ideas will be 'borrowed' by the government. (That was certainly the case in the run-up to the 2005 general election when it seemed to us Labour mimicked every popular proposal Michael Howard made.) But the media isn't much interested in these preliminaries so generating positive coverage during the process of a policy review or the preparation of a manifesto is extremely difficult.

Third, opposition parties who have recently been ejected from government inevitably bring with them a great deal of unpopularity and baggage – and, almost always, hostility in large parts of the media. A government at the end of its days falls out with old friends and makes enemies across the print and broadcast media. By the time of the 2010 election, for instance, the Labour government was left only with its faithful friends at the *Mirror* to act as cheerleader. Virtually all other relationships had been strained and broken. The task of rebuilding contacts, confidence and trust takes a very long time, so oppositions are likely to be hampered for some time by being out of touch and out of favour with the people they need to help them project themselves.

Fourth, another consequence of being in opposition is – of course – that because you have fewer MPs, and probably far fewer local councils at least for a while, there are large parts of the country where you have no one to act as local spokesmen for regional broadcast and print media. After 1997, the Conservatives were ejected from Scotland, Wales and most of the big urban areas which meant that the Party had no way of getting its message across effectively at the local level. Today, Labour is absent from much of the south and west, and from East Anglia. Local TV, radio and newspapers will not be hearing Labour voices.

Fifth, the broadcast media is vital to the process of political recovery for an opposition, as it is the only way to reach a mass audience. Newspapers play a key role in setting the news agenda, but it is TV which delivers the images which shape people's perception. By and large, however, TV news and political programmes are only really interested in hearing from the leader of the opposition. You can offer them shadow spokesmen day in and day out, but it is only the party leader who will be guaranteed the air time. And that causes two systemic problems. One, it is difficult to get coverage for other key players, leading to the attack that all opposition parties suffer from – that they are 'one man bands'. And two, because the party leader so often has to talk about a story in order to get broadcast coverage, he or she is always likely to be prone to charges of 'opportunism'. All too often, we had to put Michael Howard on the radio or television simply to get a positive story, or an attack on the government, some coverage. Otherwise there was, literally, radio silence. But that made it all too easy for Labour unfairly to say that he was an 'opportunist' who couldn't see a bandwagon without jumping onto it – the inevitable result of the way the broadcast media, outside of election times, operates.

Finally, there is the battle of the grids. Opposition parties tend to think that they must work to the 'grid' and push stories that they think are of interest. But it doesn't work that way. It is governments, with their ability to generate huge amounts of policy, of images, of news announcements, and to co-ordinate them centrally, that have command of the news grid, and there is nothing that an opposition party can do to change that. Until an election looms, and questions of balance enter news schedules, oppositions inevitably end up marching to a government's tune – with, again, the unfair implication that they are simply being tactical and opportunistic.

These are simple realities – and, just as Enoch Powell remarked, it would be absurd for a sailor to complain about the sea; these are tides with which oppositions just have to swim. But there are a number of things that oppositions must do to mitigate this, and – while recognising that there are no quick fixes – begin over time to more effectively manage the media.

Perhaps the most important of these is to understand the power of long-term relationships. In the media, it is trust and confidence that always wins the day, but these are not assets that can be stockpiled overnight. It takes time to win friends, especially among those who are not natural allies, and the job of connecting with those parts of the media that once seemed out of reach is the single most important task for a party in opposition. It takes patience, and needs to be conducted away from the day to day fracas of *Today* or newspaper headlines, and not just with the lobby, but with editors and publishers too.

If that is the most pressing task, another is to try to ensure that the selection of candidates takes place as soon as is practical, because they will plug the geographical media divide I described earlier. If there are no MPs and pitifully few councillors in a particular region, candidates will be able to provide a voice. All the experience from the 2005 and 2010 elections for the Conservatives showed that candidates selected earlier did not just stand a better chance of winning but were able to leverage local media in their own area to the benefit of the Party nationally.

Indeed, the importance of the local regional press and broadcast media to a party in opposition can't be overstated. It has a very wide reach – over 20 million people still read a local newspaper, despite a number of closures in recent years – and local broadcast TV is widely watched, too. And above all it is the most trusted medium. Getting a message across locally is by far the most effective campaigning tool, and any opposition party should make that a priority. That will often mean party leaders and senior spokesmen spending time out of London, conducting forums, doing interviews and immersing themselves in local issues. It is time-consuming, and it can often seem far away from the hurly burly of Westminster, but it is hugely important, as David Cameron showed with his successful town hall meetings during his time in opposition.

Local media campaigning is a win-win for oppositions: not only does it help you get your message across, but you find out what is of *real* concern to local people outside the M25 beltway. When Michael Howard was party leader, he would often do a readers' forum under the auspices of a local newspaper and by far our most effective campaigning ideas – on issues like cleaner hospitals and school discipline – sprang from the real concerns voiced in those local communities.

They are, in my view, much more effective than focus groups – and much cheaper!

Local papers are a vital part of the media mix, and so too are magazines and trade publications. As oppositions form policies, and seek views, they are unlikely to receive much national press attention. But industry publications and consumer magazines, both in print and online, will always be interested in ideas, and in the nuts and bolts of policy renewal. They are a clever, targeted way to reach people on subjects which are very close to their hearts – namely, their jobs and their livelihood. And as with the local press it is a win-win scenario. Not only can you talk directly to people with a specific interest in a subject, you can draw on their knowledge and pick up important policy points which will improve the finished product.

Of similar importance in the digital age is the use of new technologies to reach the widest possible audience, including many young people for whom the traditional media seems old-fashioned and outmoded. This can work on many levels. First of all, newspapers and magazines are all now digital enterprises where content is king. Using the power of their websites – which have far higher audiences than traditional printed products – is of real value. Far too many times I still hear political colleagues only interested in getting an article printed in the paper. Yes, it looks good, but far more people will see it if it is on a widely read website. But second, and perhaps more importantly, opposition parties can use the internet – especially now there is such widespread broadband penetration – to get their message across unfiltered and unalloyed by commentators. Interactive websites, online campaigns, blogs, viral emails – particularly using audio-visual material – all get straight to the voter.

Between 2005 and 2010 David Cameron's Conservatives pioneered a new way of campaigning with *WebCameron*, an innovative, modern and highly successful way of getting the message out to a new audience. But in many ways, that was in the foothills of what can be achieved – and we are still some way behind the United States where digital campaigning made a real difference to the Democrats in opposition before the 2008 presidential and congressional elections.

Despite the best efforts to win new audiences through local and digital media, the national broadcast media will still be of great importance to an opposition – but, as I mentioned, their tendency always to gravitate to the party leader is fraught with problems. There is no quick fix here, but it will always be prudent early on in a parliament to identify just three or four people whose faces can represent the party, and then to push them to the broadcasters as much as possible over months and years. It is no good pretending that you will be able to get air time for the two dozen members of the shadow Cabinet. But over a five-year parliament it should be possible to ensure that a few faces become familiar, household names. This is in essence what Tony Blair did in the years between 1994 and 1997, by building up the television personalities of just a handful of the New Labour hierarchy – namely Gordon Brown, John Prescott, Mo Mowlam and Robin Cook – rather than a much wider group. By the time of the 1997 election, Labour was not just perceived as a 'one man band', a problem that springs from having a strong and telegenic leader.

Finally, there is the issue of the 'grid'. The production of grids can become a great obsession for opposition parties as they try to drag a reluctant news media onto their territory. Yet it often ends as a frustrating failure, because oppositions will seldom have the ability to consistently make the news. Of course, activities need to be planned properly and in a coherent manner, but oppositions need to be fleet of foot and ready to change their plans at a moment's notice to ride the issues of the day. During the 2005 general election I recall a number of press conferences that we ran on issues like government waste or MRSA which all went completely unreported because the news agenda had moved on – to Iraq. Not one of our strongest issues, there was an unwillingness to follow the story, which meant that we ceased to be part of it. And that, for any opposition, is lethal.

None of this is quick, or easy, but – provided they are prepared to begin work soon after an election defeat – oppositions do generally have the luxury of time. Time to build long-term relationships, even in unfamiliar territory. Time to understand and invest in the power of digital. Time to tour the country and plug into the real concerns of real people. Time to build up a brand, and the faces and images that underpin it. None of these are things, however, that can be left to the last years of the parliament. By then, even the best media minds would be able only to utter those two saddest words in politics: 'too late.'

9. Revolutionary Foot Soldiers: A Researcher's Tale

Nigel Fletcher

So much for the theory and the history, but what about the day job of opposing the government? My own experience, which developed into a lasting fascination with the concept of opposition, was gained from the lower ranks of the operation, working first in Parliament as a researcher for a shadow Cabinet member, and then as an adviser in the Conservative Research Department for four and a half years.

Walking each morning into Conservative HQ (still at 32 Smith Square when I joined, but soon moved to 25 Victoria Street, then to 30 Millbank), I was often struck by a slightly surreal feeling. Here was a reception desk, then an open-plan office with rows of desks, computers, some photocopiers and a water cooler. People made tea in the kitchen, chatted to one another and opened their emails. Looking at this very ordinary scene, we could have been selling insurance, or running the distribution operation of a moderately successful electronics company. Instead, we were trying to bring down the government. To me, this audacious mission statement sat oddly with the mundane world of IT helpdesks and air conditioning vents.

The fact that this whole operation could proceed unhindered in such an unremarkable setting is perhaps the best outward sign of a free and functioning democracy. In countries where opposition is not free, such activity would be highly dangerous, and its supporters subject to intimidation

– or worse – by state authorities. They would meet in basement rooms, communicate by covert methods, and try to evade detection by the police. The Conservative Party's staff in opposition, by contrast, commuted to work, spent the day undermining the government, then went home (or to the pub). It was a very British form of revolutionary activity.

But revolutionary it certainly was. The setting may have been ordinary enough, but in the 'war-room' (as the combined press and research offices were always known), there was unmistakeably a war in progress – complete with battle-plans and top secret information to keep out of enemy hands. Before the 2005 election Lord Saatchi, the then co-Chairman of the Party, told us we should think of ourselves like the Bletchley Park code-breakers, refusing to discuss our work at all with friends on the outside. When an embarrassing leak occurred soon after, we were summoned to a meeting in the press conference room, where the offending newspaper article was projected on the screen as a backdrop to a stern lecture on discipline.

There were attempts to infiltrate our headquarters, too. On a couple of occasions undercover reporters were caught trying to gain access to, or even employment in, various departments. One of these – which took place after the move to 30 Millbank – was foiled in spectacular fashion by press officers, who embarked on a counter-espionage operation of which our neighbours at MI5 headquarters would have been proud. I would love to tell you how they did it, but then someone would have to kill you.

My own piece of sub-James Bond intelligence activity came during the 2005 election, after our Treasury spokesman Howard Flight had been infamously caught out making overblown and unhelpful remarks about the extent of public spending reductions. The comments had been recorded at a meeting of the Thatcherite Conservative Way Forward group at a bar somewhere in central London, and its organisers were deeply embarrassed that their meeting had been infiltrated and caused such problems. They had their suspicions about who the culprit may have been, as a rather distinctive-looking young man had been spotted in the audience. Someone thought they recognised him as a Labour student, but no one knew his name. I took on the job of tracking him down, and my mole hunt soon came up with a name, which we were indeed able to link to Labour. This was duly briefed to a newspaper as evidence of a 'dirty tricks' operation by our opponents, and the individual in question even found himself subjected to an investigation by Michael Crick on *Newsnight*, during which he strongly denied being the mole.

Such incidents were merely diverting skirmishes on the fringes of battle, but they had their place in the wider campaign. At all times, we knew our main objective was to attack the government and promote our own policies. The balance between these two strands of opposition – opposing and proposing – was not always easy to maintain. Many shadow ministers were keener to have their research staff working on developing policy in their area, and saw the constant demand from Party HQ for political attacks as a secondary consideration. Others were natural oppositionists, keen to get one over on Labour, and less interested in their own policy. In truth, of course, both are vital functions, but it was not always easy to manage the two priorities. This balancing act is one of the big strategic issues facing a leader and shadow Cabinet, but for the backroom staff, it was a daily issue of time management, and of trying to serve different masters.

On the attack side, there were tried and tested ways of going about the job. By far the biggest of these when I joined the Research Department in 2004 was the written parliamentary question (WPQ). In consultation with our shadow ministers we would draft suggested questions to the government on a range of subjects, which would then be signed off or amended by MPs in our frontbench team and tabled. These were usually aimed at getting detailed and up-to-date information about the performance of a department of state, with the intention of showing the government failing to meet its targets or generally performing badly.

Sometimes they threw up new and interesting information, but often they simply acted as a way of reinforcing an attack we were already using. In my own field of education, for example, we knew that truancy was rising, and that the number of pupils reaching the expected level in English and maths was too low. We said it often in speeches and in interviews, but it was rarely considered news. The challenge was to find a new way of presenting the information – and the phrase 'New figures uncovered by the Conservatives' sometimes did the trick on a slow news day, when a reply to a WPQ could be presented as new, even if the information in it wasn't.

A really good attack story required some more ingenious thinking, however. We couldn't count on specialist reporters to be fooled by 'new figures' when they had seen them dozens of times already. So questions could better be used to gather detailed information over a period of time, which could then be analysed and built up into a much bigger picture. Regional and local data was a very good resource – as well as showing disparities in performance across the country, it also provided the basis for local press releases which could be used by candidates and MPs in their own areas. In education this was dangerous territory: with so many local education authorities run by Conservatives, there was a risk we would expose poor performances by our colleagues. I was always fairly robust about such things – if a Conservative council had failing schools, it merely strengthened the case for our policy of setting schools free of local authorities, whoever was in control of them. They didn't always see it quite like that.

This type of analysis could, however, reveal much politically useful information. I was once able to demonstrate that the first planned waves of school refurbishments under the Building

Schools for the Future programme involved overwhelmingly Labour local authorities. This story got some good coverage in one of the broadsheets, and the Chairman of the Education Select Committee even put the charge to the Schools Minister Jim Knight when he appeared before them shortly afterwards. The Minister retorted that of all the daft stories he'd seen in newspapers, this one took the biscuit. I was rather proud of that accolade.

As well as seeking performance data, WPQs were also a good tool for extracting embarrassing nuggets of information. There were several themes that played well in the media: government waste and ministerial grandeur were amongst the most prominent. Requests for the total amount paid to management consultants, the cost of office refurbishments, ministerial travel arrangements and so on all provided useful ammunition. 'Round-robin' questions to all departments could yield excellent results, and were often tabled at the instigation of the political unit in the Research Department. Free of policy and departmental concerns, this elite squad of professional cynics cheerfully spent their days plotting new lines of attack. Headlines like 'Whitehall spends millions on pot plants' were their everyday objective, and were frequently achieved.

Revelations like these were often saved up to be deployed when they would have most impact. Press officers and researchers were encouraged to build up supplies of self-contained, pre-packaged stories to be released over Christmas or during the summer recess, when other political news was in short supply. Some achieved excellent coverage (known, in the vocabulary of battle, as 'media hits'), whilst others failed to take off at all. Several of my Christmas breaks were marred when I saw my carefully gift-wrapped seasonal offerings had failed to excite the nation's news desks. But, like the turkeys they doubtless were, they were able to be reheated and served up again at a later date.

During my time in the Research Department, a new

tool became available that was to change significantly how we went about such political operations. The Freedom of Information (FOI) Act opened up huge new possibilities for gaining information about the workings of government, and embarrassing ministers in the process. Shortly after it came into force I requested the minutes of the Department for Education and Skills' weekly board meetings, at which senior officials reported on their activity. It took many months and an exchange of letters with the Permanent Secretary before I was able to extract a partial release of the documents, but they provided an invaluable insight into the workings of the Department, and prompted many follow-up enquiries.

Those of my colleagues who were most adept at using FOI increased their 'hit' rate markedly. The most effective method was to use it in conjunction with parliamentary questions to delve deeper behind the answers given. So, a question might be tabled asking what guidance a department had given to its staff on a particular issue. The answer from the minister might mention a handbook or staff policy that was issued regularly, and this would then be requested under FOI, along with previous versions. This might show that a staff policy had been changed, with procedures perhaps slackened or some criteria made less demanding. If that were in the field of, say, social security, then bingo! 'Ministers order secret amnesty for benefit cheats.' Or a question could be asked about meetings a minister had had with a particular organisation, and after receiving the answer, the minutes of the meeting would be requested ('government holds secret talks on…'). It could be a long process, but when it worked it could yield excellent results. 'New figures uncovered by the Conservatives' increasingly gave way to 'Documents obtained under the Freedom of Information Act reveal…'

One frustration we all experienced was the occasional grumble from backbench MPs or party members that 'we never see anything in the papers' from our team. I can't have been the only adviser to have been taken to task for inactivity by an activist who waved the *Daily Mail* at me, saying 'Look at all this about kids not being taught history properly – why aren't you shouting about that?' More often than not, the story we should have been 'shouting about' was one we had placed there in the first place. Annoying though this was, it was actually a mark of success – if a negative story about the government had lodged itself in the complainant's mind, it was a sure sign it would have registered with other readers too. As Ronald Reagan was fond of saying, there's no limit to what you can achieve if you don't mind who gets the credit.

Was this serious opposition, or cheap political point-scoring? Some of it was clearly rather silly, and some shadow ministers thought it beneath their dignity to indulge in such games. Others perhaps took it too far themselves. But it was an important part of keeping up pressure on ministers and creating a narrative that the government was failing and making mistakes. Attracting media coverage is not easy, and it was often the small or quirky stories that caught the imagination of newspapers, rather than the more serious data analysis. But as long as the story illustrated a wider point, it was worth doing. So lavish expenditure was usually fair game, and indeed some of the stories about government waste have resurfaced since the coalition took office, used as indications of expenditure which cannot now be justified.

You will have seen from the above, incidentally, that we in the Research Department worked very closely with our colleagues in the press office. It was indeed a close working relationship, but the two institutions remained proudly independent of one another. The Conservative Research Department, founded in 1929 by Neville Chamberlain, had been based in a separate building until 1979, and part of that mindset remained. The sense of history was reinforced by the formidable presence of Alistair B. Cooke (recently ennobled as Lord Lexden), who had joined the Department in 1977 to work for Airey Neave on Northern Ireland policy, and later became its deputy Director and editor of the general election reference tome *The Campaign Guide* (more of that later). He left following the 1997 general election, but returned in 2004 when Michael Howard reconstituted the CRD.

It needed reconstitution, because under Iain Duncan Smith's leadership there had been an experiment with 'hybrid' political officers, who were meant to cover both press and research functions. The experiment was not thought a success, and on becoming leader, Michael Howard moved swiftly to re-establish a Research Department separate from the press office. It was in the resulting recruitment drive that I found myself swept into the shabby functionality of 32 Smith Square, then in its final few months as the Party's HQ.

Press and research may have been separate, but they remained physically close, being located alongside one another in the 'war-room'. This arrangement was, however, subject to change in what became a regular pattern. After a while, it was decided that what was needed was for the press and research officers for individual frontbench teams to be more closely integrated, so the seating arrangements (though not the management structures) were changed so that, for example, the health, education and transport advisers were sat facing their relevant press officers. This certainly made sense, given that we worked most closely with one another, but it soon became clear the arrangement was not without problems. Press officers required TV monitors tuned to 24-hour news, whilst their telephone extensions were linked to enable any of them to pick up calls to the main press office number. The result – a cacophony of ringing phones, blaring headlines and loud phone conversations – was not always the best backdrop for the work of researchers.

So after a year or so, it was decided that what was really needed was for the CRD to be sat together again in one bloc, and the press office to be gathered together at the other end of the office. This co-location/separation dance was performed several times during the few years I was in post. We also moved offices altogether from Smith Square to Victoria Street, then in 2006 CRD officers were scattered to the four corners of the parliamentary estate, before being brought back together with the rest of CCHQ at 30 Millbank. All in all, I lost count of how many different desks I occupied.

Throughout this game of musical chairs, the CRD maintained its identity and the idiosyncratic air that has pervaded since its foundation. This is not the place for a study of the history and character of this fine institution, which has in any case been effectively described in the book *Tory Policy-Making*, published for the Department's eightieth anniversary in 2009. Edited by Alistair Cooke, this contained contributions from former staffers Michael Dobbs, Chris Patten, Oliver Letwin and someone called David Cameron. The latter's essay cited Harold Macmillan's former Private Secretary John Wyndham, who described a 'bohemian sort of efficiency', which neatly encapsulates what I found during my time there. Cameron's own description of what he found in the late 1980s also rings true. 'I will always associate CRD with an ordered sort of chaos' he wrote, before going on to describe how he quickly learnt the skills to meet the rigorous standards expected for briefing notes and speeches.

Whilst media 'hits' were part of our job, and were increasingly demanded as elections drew nearer, they were only one side of our work. Without the machine of a Whitehall department to support them, shadow ministers have to rely on their party staff for a whole range of their opposition functions, and the Research Department at such times has become a form of shadow civil service. This role is of course much more important in opposition than in government, and presents researchers at an early stage in their careers with opportunities to have significant responsibility and access to frontline politicians. This is of course a great privilege and an exciting opportunity for young, politically interested young graduates, but can equally be very daunting.

Those of us who were Special Advisers for a particular subject would often receive phone calls asking for guidance on Party policy in our area of responsibility, conversations which would usually begin: 'What's our line on…?' These might be from an MP's staff, prospective candidates or, occasionally, from senior politicians themselves. In this way, I found myself advising an impatient Ann Widdecombe about testing policy, William Hague about university fees and, on one occasion, answering my mobile whilst on the concourse of Manchester Piccadilly station to find myself talking to Michael Heseltine, who was in search of a 'killer fact' on school standards.

Such encounters were of course memorable, particularly when the person asking the questions is a famous figure from a past government. But what is remarkable in retrospect is not who was advised, but the fact I was trusted to advise them in the first place. If government is about what you do, opposition is about what you say, so 'the line' is all-important. Being able to respond to such enquiries promptly requires a pretty detailed knowledge of your brief, and of agreed policy or, in many cases, the holding line we were taking whilst developing policy. Gaps in your knowledge were swiftly shown up, and the embarrassment of having to say 'I'm not sure, I'll have to get back to you' was incentive enough to do your homework.

We may have been the designated experts on them, but where did such 'lines to take' come from? We obviously were not plucking them from thin air, but neither were we reciting them all from an agreed encyclopedia of policy. The reality, as ever, is complex and rather fluid. On major issues, Party policy will be clear, and is likely to have been the subject of keynote speeches and declarations from the Party leader and senior spokespersons. All of these will have been cleared by shadow Cabinet (or were supposed to have been). A policy document may have been produced, and will have been drafted and redrafted to ensure the language is agreed by all. As policy advisers, we would usually be heavily involved in this process, and thus have got to know the political significance of each disputed phrase, and why a particular reference had been left ambiguous or phrased in a certain way.

We would usually also prepare a 'hostile Q&A' document, designed to answer the most likely criticisms and attacks on the policy, or at least provide the language agreed for rebutting the claim. An extensive version of this document would usually serve to fill in most gaps in the detail, and would often be held back as an internal document, rather than published. The combination of these documents provided most of the lines we needed to respond to queries on our policy.

For our critique of government policy, however, a different sort of document came into play: the CRD brief. Not intended for publication, these were working files for use by frontbenchers, other advisers and anyone else who needed briefing on an issue. In education, I would have full background briefs on standards, the exam system, school discipline, higher education and so on. These would begin with a 'top line' summary of our position on the issue, of perhaps a couple of sentences, then a list of bullet points containing the other key points we would wish to make. These would be a combination of attacks on the government's record and approach and more positive proposals of our own.

The rest of the brief would contain the detailed background to the issue, designed to allow someone to go from having no prior knowledge of it to knowing all the politically relevant history and debating points. This would include the main measures the government had enacted, key quotes from ministers setting out their position, and useful quotes from relevant organisations and individuals. All of this would be backed up by relevant data showing the government's performance, and allowing the reader to get a clear picture of the facts on the subject. It also needed to give the full background to our alternative proposals, with statements from Conservative spokesmen and a battery of helpful quotes from credible external experts backing up our position. As time went on, new lines of attack opened up and our policy developed, with the briefs growing ever more detailed. But they had to remain absolutely up-to-date, with redundant material removed and new developments covered, or they were no use.

These rolling briefs were the backbone of our briefing operation, but in themselves they were often too unwieldy and detailed for general use. Each week, however, the CRD produced a document made up of more succinct briefs on all main topical issues, which was sent out at the weekend to key people, having also been used to help prepare frontbenchers for appearances on the BBC's *Question Time* and *Any Questions*. These would consist of a couple of pages at most on each issue, with a set of hostile questions and answers at the end. They were often quite challenging to produce, with complex issues having to be condensed down and only the best material included.

Sometimes more specific briefs were required, such as when the leader did a major or specialist interview. An appearance by Michael Howard on BBC Radio One's *Newsbeat* during the 2005 election, for example, would involve researchers collating key facts on current soap plots, pop music and other matters thought likely to arise in a bulletin aimed at a youth audience. He needed no briefing on football, being an avid fan of the sport (particularly of Liverpool FC), and I suspect such 'pop culture' briefs as a whole were done more to demonstrate our efficiency than because he needed them. But they provided some light relief when they arose. A few years ago the BBC comedy *The Thick of It* showed their fictional minister being given a 'zeitgeist' tape to watch in similar circumstances, but as far as I know we never went that far.

The fact the opposition's job is more reactive than proactive meant that 'lines to take' were most often generated as a result of something the government had done, and the expectation that shadow ministers would have an instant comment. These responses followed a set pattern – a minister would put out a press release, or a journalist would ask for a response to a story they were working on. These would generally be passed on to us by our press colleagues, who sought a draft quote for us to put out. If the issue was familiar they could draft it themselves, but otherwise we would have to help them out. Once it had been done, the process of clearing it with a shadow spokesman would begin. If the issue was high-profile we would want it put out in the name of our shadow Secretary of State, and in most cases it was preferable to put it to them first, even if it was going to be put out in the name of a junior colleague.

Deciding in whose name a quote was issued became a matter of judgement, and sensitivity to political egos within the frontbench team was always required. Most shadow ministers had a defined area of responsibility, and could resent it if they felt their boss was always muscling in on their patch, and other members of the team could feel neglected if a colleague was constantly hogging the limelight. Usually it was much more practical than that – a suggested draft was sent round by email, and it was a matter of who replied soonest or who was available when the press officer tried to call them. Those who never answered their phone or replied to email were the ones who found their press appearances most restricted. On some issues it was a routine process, but where it was more contentious, several amended drafts began to fly around and a debate would ensue, with varying degrees of seriousness. One of my shadow Secretaries of State once emailed back, 'I literally can't bring myself to care about this one way or the other', and delegated it to a shadow minister to reply.

Care always had to be taken, though, because these lines, once issued, could be cited as definitive statements of Party policy. If we or our boss got it wrong, we could ultimately find ourselves being overruled by the leader's office, and a humiliating 'clarification' issued, which would of course become a story in itself. Another danger was a shadow minister who disagreed with an agreed position trying their luck by redrafting a quote to support their view. Getting them back on message was a diplomatic challenge, and sometimes couldn't be achieved without the intervention of the shadow Secretary of State. This always made me feel like a sneak telling tales to teacher, an impression reinforced by the reaction from those overruled.

Sometimes it was decided we would rather not comment on a story for some reason, in which case it was a matter either of telling that frankly to a journalist, or of giving them a quote of such crushing blandness that they couldn't possibly use it. Where we did want to be quoted, the maxim that 'speed kills' was drummed into us, and it was a matter of professional pride how quickly we could devise an eye-catching response, get it cleared and issued. If it was a big story, the Press Association newswire would add the quote to their coverage, and getting it up there before the Lib Dems' response was a prized objective.

The need for a speedy response could require an innovative approach. On one occasion my shadow Secretary of State was due to take off on a long-haul flight in the morning, and would be out of contact until the evening. Knowing that a government announcement was due, we discussed our probable line, but with some crucial details not available, we couldn't clear it in advance. Eventually, and with mock gravitas, he told his Chief of Staff and me that we had 'powers plenipotentiary' to issue the first response to the news whilst he was in the air. The announcement came, and we drafted a quote, which duly went out in his name. As it flashed up on the newswire, I reflected that we had been party to a minor coup d'état. Certainly there were some in CCHQ who seemed to think the system would work much better without democratically elected politicians slowing things down.

At the opposite end of the scale from these short instant responses was the CRD's flagship publication, *The Campaign Guide*. This weighty 'blue bible' pre-dates even the Department itself, having first appeared in 1892, and has thus become a much-cherished CRD institution. Published ahead of a general election, it contains detailed analysis from the Conservative perspective of current policy issues, along with information about how the Party would approach them. Its audience is the thousands of candidates and activists on the streets who need to be able to lay their hands on authoritative and useful material to answer any question thrown at them on the doorsteps, in public meetings or interviews. The 2005 edition, to which I contributed, ran to more than 700 pages, and maintained the tradition of being printed in a tall, narrow volume, ideal for flicking through quickly on the move.

The process of drafting this impressive tome was overseen by CRD veteran Alistair Cooke, who had returned to the Department as Editor-in-Chief. His strictures on the correct way to write a brief were a masterclass which all researchers had to learn quickly. If our text was not succinct or clearly enough expressed, or used clichés and jargon, we would face schoolmasterly disapproval as the draft was savaged by the editor's pen. Quotes and data had to be rigorously sourced, with references cited accurately and consistently, in line with CRD house style. This high standard was demanded of all substantive briefing material, but none more so than *The Campaign Guide*. This had its own distinct style, so there was no question of cutting and pasting text from existing briefs – it all had to be redrafted from scratch. The result was an impressive document of which I think we were all proud.

In addition to churning out documents, lines to take and assorted other briefing material, as advisers in opposition we did of course find ourselves called upon to fulfil the more generic roles of a political aide: fetching and carrying documents, tracking down obscure quotes for speeches, and the essential modern skill of talking urgently into a mobile phone whilst walking alongside the boss and looking important.

We would also meet delegations of people our superiors didn't have the time or inclination to see. This duty was a telling one – in the early years of opposition, few people were interested in meeting us, and it could even be difficult to secure meetings for our shadow ministers with senior figures in the public and private sectors. After 2005, as our poll rating grew, requests for meetings flowed in as senior executives and assorted other people fell over themselves to get an appointment. Those of us with long memories could see which the fair-weather friends were, and which had been willing to engage when power was a distant prospect. The public affairs woman who cheerfully announced 'We've decided it's definitely worth talking to you guys now' clearly didn't realise how cynical their attitude appeared to those of us who had endured years of being ignored by her profession.

Nevertheless, meeting with as many relevant people as you can whilst in opposition is undoubtedly a good idea. Not only does it promote goodwill, but it provides you with vital inside knowledge of how government policy is operating in practice, and suggests lines of enquiry and attack which can be followed up. Better still, taking up invitations to visit organisations on the frontline of your policy brief is an invaluable learning experience. Too often, pressure of time means this is not possible, and as an adviser I found much of my experience of visiting schools restricted to attending policy launch events, which with the media in tow are not conducive to seeing much of what goes on.

Shadow ministers in general manage to make many such visits on their own without media present, and I wish I had managed to get out of the office and accompany them more often. When David Cameron was shadow Education Secretary he visited Wandsworth Prison to see how their prisoner literacy programme worked, and as it was relatively near the office I was able to tag along. There were no cameras or press, and David's entourage consisted of just me and another staff member from his office. We met with the Governor, sat in on one of the literacy classes, spoke to prisoners in their cells, and saw for ourselves the other work that prison staff and charity volunteers were doing. It was one of the most fascinating experiences of my time on the education brief, and had a lasting effect on a number of aspects of policy. Shadow ministers and their staff would be well advised to use the anonymity and freedom of opposition to do as much of this low-key fact-finding as they can.

The job of a researcher in opposition can be tough and stressful. The pressures and responsibilities you face are often equivalent to those faced by senior government officials, and you seemingly have none of their advantages or resources to help deal with them. But it is also a huge opportunity, and a privilege to be so closely involved in politics at a high level. The writer Ferdinand Mount was working in the Research Department when the Conservatives lost the 1964 election, and was told his experience of working with frontbenchers would now change: 'You'll find it much more fun now they've got nobody to look after them' an enthusiastic colleague informed him.[1]

That remark contains a basic truth that remains true today. The job is serious and demanding, but the experience of being part of a small team working together in adversity promotes a sense of real camaraderie, and makes the hard work and long hours worthwhile.

---

1. Ferdinand Mount, *Cold Cream: My Life and other Mistakes* (Bloomsbury, 2008)

I said at the start of this chapter that 'bringing down the government' was a peculiar day job, and it is. But that is really only the negative side of the job description. With equally lofty ambition, the positive side of opposition could be summed up as 'trying to change the world.' That is surely something worth doing for a few years.

Endnote

There is no definitive handbook for being in opposition. In many ways there cannot be, and this volume has not seriously tried to fulfil that role. Every situation is different, and as in wider politics, events lay waste to the best laid plans. But, simply by attempting to piece together snippets of advice and historical guidance, it has hopefully become clear there are themes which recur in each period of opposition. From these, there are some general lessons:

Get organised: The way you arrange your office and your working patterns are more fluid in opposition, but they are crucial to your success. Without the structure and expertise provided by the civil service, you must build an effective and high-calibre team yourself. Getting it wrong can cripple your operation. Just ask Iain Duncan Smith.

Choose your weapons wisely: An opposition cannot compete with the government on resources, so you must be inventive. In what is a David and Goliath contest, you can use the advantages of greater agility to aim your slingshot where it can do most damage. Parliamentary ambushes, media attacks and effective research will wear down ministers and help expose their mistakes.

Have a strategy and stick to it: The most successful leaders are those who have adopted a systematic formula for repositioning their party to reconnect with the electorate. This can be tough, but departing from it almost always ends in failure, and puts you at the mercy of party factions and of events.

Be a government-in-waiting: Knee-jerk opposition and political street-fighting have their place, but must be balanced with your other crucial role – the public must see you as a viable alternative administration. That means maintaining discipline, ensuring you present a credible policy platform (whilst not rushing to publish excessive detail), and preparing yourself properly for power. This is not complacency, it is a constitutional duty.

Cheer up, or it might never happen: The predominant feelings of those in opposition have historically been of frustration, and even misery. But there is no point wallowing in despair. You have a job to do here and now, and it is an important one for our democracy – quite apart from any future you may have in government. As with most jobs, adopting a positive attitude to your current position and doing it well will increase your chances of promotion.

The official status of Her Majesty's Loyal Opposition gives rise both to the duties it must fulfil and the resources to which it is entitled. But the gap between them serves merely to reinforce the inadequacy of the position facing each leader and shadow Cabinet. This is troublesome for them, but it should also be troubling for us as citizens.

Despite the many mechanisms which are now in place to allow us to hold our government accountable – the increased openness brought by the Freedom of Information Act and the current coalition's stated commitment to publishing more detailed material – armchair auditing can only augment the scrutiny role of Parliament. It cannot replace it. The opposition therefore retains a fundamental role in defending our hard-won freedoms, and ensuring the proper functioning of our democracy between elections.

When those elections do occur, the choice facing us as voters is shaped and framed by how well the opposition has fulfilled the other half of its role – that of providing a credible alternative government. If its shadow ministers have failed politically, they will fail to convince the electorate to trust them with power, perhaps leaving an imperfect and tired government in place. But if they succeed politically whilst failing on effective policy formation, the government of our country will be even more ill served as unprepared ministers enact bad policy.

'How to be in opposition' is therefore not just a topic of self-serving interest to politicians. It is essential to ensuring we are better governed, in both the short and longer term. Huge resources are put into developing better practice in government, both at the administrative and policy levels, to try to prevent bad policy outcomes. But there is nothing remotely comparable to prevent such outcomes arising from the performance of the opposition. The establishment of the Centre for Opposition Studies is a response to that perceived deficiency, and we will do what we can to prompt greater consideration of these issues. In the end, however, the onus to make adequate official provision for this opposition's constitutional role falls on Parliament, and on the government which holds sway there.

Just as with the provision of a salary, a car and 'Short Money', any significant move to strengthen arrangements for the opposition will need the approval of those they are trying to displace. A wise government should see the value of a 'formidable opposition' (in Disraeli's phrase) and see its achievement as an important priority. What might this involve?

Greater state funding is not the only answer. All the Short Money in the world will not lead automatically to a more effective shadow government. The form that assistance takes is as important a consideration. The introduction of a policy development grant, paid in the same way as existing funds, was limited in its imagination. The sort of innovation needed is in the field of expertise and structure, not raw cash.

Secondment of civil servants is an obvious suggestion, and one which has been floated from time to time. It brings with it problems of how to maintain the proper independence of the opposition and neutrality of such officials, but these should be possible to resolve. Whilst it is difficult to completely separate the purely political activity of an opposition party from its official duties, it is a distinction which is managed in legislatures abroad, and indeed in relation to the party of government in the UK.

It cannot be right that an incoming leader finds they have to begin with a completely blank sheet of paper in terms of organisation and office support. Some key positions must be filled by trusted aides and political advisers, but there are many staff members whose jobs, like those in government, continue whoever the incumbent opposition are. Correspondence secretaries and office administrators would fall into this category, but more specialist posts could also conceivably be filled by high-flying civil servants. As a bare minimum, a Private Secretary on secondment from the Cabinet Office would enable there to be an authoritative link to the official machine on such matters as foreign visits, meetings with visiting dignitaries and sensitive official briefings.

Alternatively, an official 'Office of HM Opposition' could be established within Parliament with specialist permanent staff combined with party appointees. If such an office were clearly identified as a parliamentary institution, it would underline the proper distinction between the executive and the legislative brake on its power. We only have to look at the excellent House of Commons Library researchers to see how formidable such an institution could be, without needing to be partisan. None of this need tie the hands of the leader in shaping their policy-making and campaigning structures, which would rightly remain party functions. But if we accept there are some predominantly parliamentary and official duties inherent in opposition, it makes little sense to force each new leader to reinvent the wheel, with varying degrees of success. The public should expect the best possible support for those who are charged with speaking up for them, and this is not always guaranteed under the current arrangements.

Whatever changes and reforms may be made, some aspects of opposition will remain constant. The shock of losing office will always be profound, and the road back will seem dauntingly long. But as I hope this book has shown, life in the shadows need not be as dark as it first appears.

Epilogue

Nigel Fletcher

During the 2010 general election I returned to Conservative Campaign HQ to help out in the media monitoring section of the press office, working the early morning shift each day from 5.30a.m. It was a minor role, but I had wanted to play my part in the culmination of our long years in opposition.

Over the five days of negotiations which followed the election result I watched, along with the rest of the country, as the new government took shape. I was in Parliament on the Tuesday when those developments reached their conclusion, and saw the comings and goings which led to the coalition being formed.

In the minutes following Gordon Brown's resignation I met up with some friends from the Conservative Party events team, who had just had the unenviable task of managing the media scrum as William Hague, George Osborne and Oliver Letwin returned from the Cabinet Office to Parliament. We were standing in the lobby of the Norman Shaw South building when the first visible sign of the imminent transfer of power appeared: the armoured prime ministerial Daimler arrived in the car park outside to take David Cameron to his appointment with the Queen.

Shortly afterwards, David himself came down the stairs, hand in hand with Samantha, and followed by his inner team of advisers. As I shook his hand, I meant to say 'congratulations' or 'good luck' but heard myself instead saying 'thank you'. I'm not quite sure why, but it seemed somehow appropriate.

We then watched from the top of the steps as he walked to the car and left Parliament for his last journey as leader of the opposition.

Later that night, after he had entered Downing Street as Prime Minister, I walked back through Parliament and past the shadow Cabinet room. Having previously worked in the next-door office, I had developed a somewhat curatorial attitude to it. I stopped and went inside for a last look. The chairs were scattered untidily, hastily abandoned after the meetings of the previous days. As I used to do at the end of each day, I tucked them back in neatly under the table, leaving the leader's chair (the only one with arms) pulled back so it was facing the door at a slight angle. Then I turned out the lights and shut the door behind me. After thirteen years, it was ready for a new team to take possession.

A Citizen's Guide to Electoral Reform

Alan Renwick

One thing's for sure. Elections matter. The ballot box is the only thing guaranteed to make politicians listen. Electoral rules shape the nature of our politics: the relationship between government and governed, between candidates and their parties. And what if tweaking the system could prevent MPs claiming expenses for their duck houses? The choice will be yours. The first nationwide referendum for over 35 years is on the horizon. But it's all too easy just to switch off when it comes to the debate on electoral reform.

Full of acronyms: AV, AMS, STV and MMP – it's like being plunged into an alphabet soup! *A Citizen's Guide to Electoral Reform* is here to help. This easy-to-read guide cuts through the obscurities and lets you know what's really at stake when the referendum comes.

208pp paperback • £9.99 • Available now

www.bitebackpublishing.com

So You Want To be A Politician

Shane Greer

So You Want to be a Politician is a must read for any first time candidate or anyone looking to put together and run an effective campaign at any level of public life. This accessible, practical guide offers common sense advice for almost any scenario.

Featuring contributions and advice from some of the leading names in contemporary British campaigning, *So You Want to be a Politician* is an essential resource that some of today's serving politicians could make good use of.

304pp paperback • £14.99 • Available now

www.bitebackpublishing.com

Speaking to Lead
How to make speeches that make a difference
John Shosky

As a speechwriter and consultant, John Shosky's credentials are impeccable. During the last 25 years he has worked with people at the highest levels of government and business, including three presidential administrations and many top executives from Fortune 500 companies. In this book Shosky distils his incomparable know-how into an accessible practical guide to the essentials of his art.

Speaking to Lead teaches the importance and use of speech as action: a tool to fix problems and push issues forward. As the title suggests, from the boardroom to the podium, this is a book for leaders.

288pp paperback • £14.99 • Available now

www.bitebackpublishing.com